LIFE Does Have a Purpose

'God is not far off from each one of us,' said one of his ancient servants. The aim of this book is to show that God can be readily approached, and that he desires all men to come to a knowledge of his simple requirements for a life of purpose now and to endless time. From the Scriptures and his dealings with humankind his marvelous personality and good purpose toward us are revealed.

—The Publishers

CONTENTS

CHAPTER   PAGE

1   Life *Does* Have a Purpose 5

2   God—The Generous Householder 17

3   A Paradise Home Ahead 25

4   Do We Need Rulership by God? 38

5   Why Has God Allowed Suffering on Earth? .. 48

6   God Comes to Mankind's Rescue 65

7   The Source and Sustainer of Life 77

8   Outstanding Gifts That
       Reveal the God of Love 87

9   Universal Law Reveals Purpose in Life 98

10   Does God Count You Personally Important? .. 108

11   You Can Know God's Purpose 119

12   How Far Has Preparation Progressed? 130

13   A Pattern of Things to Come 143

14   The Elimination of Crime and Injustice 156

15   The End of Sickness and Death 167

16   You Can Be Confident of a Reward 181

NOTE: Unless otherwise indicated, Bible quotations in this book
are from the modern-language *New World Translation of the
Holy Scriptures,* revised edition of 1971.

In connection with dates, the abbreviation B.C.E. means "Before
the Common Era," and C.E. means "Of the Common Era."

Chapter 1

Life *Does* Have a Purpose

HOW good it is to be alive, to feel that you are accomplishing something and that your life has real meaning! Nobody really enjoys an aimless life—a life without a purpose.

² Around the earth, millions of persons are working hard and trying to find happiness in living. Yet there comes a time when people stop and ask, Where am I really going? It may seem that life is merely a matter of living a few short years, raising children to carry on the family name, and then the children in turn repeat the same cycle. Is there no greater purpose in it all?

³ Also, people know that, all too often, an economic upset, a war or some other calamity may wipe out a whole lifetime of effort. More sadly, to lose a dearly loved one because of sickness, accident or crime can make life suddenly seem terribly empty, aimless. Even at best, life seems so short. Compared to the ageless universe around us, a human lifetime is like the mere tick of a clock.

⁴ Surely there is something better in store for mankind, something that can give true meaning to our lives. If so, what is it? To answer this question we must first get the answer to an even more basic question: Is this universe and all life

1, 2. Even if a person is living an enjoyable life, what perplexing questions may trouble him? (Ecclesiastes 1:2-4, 10, 11) 3, 4. (a) What things can quickly change the whole plan of our lives? (Psalm 90:10) (b) If we want something that will give more meaning to our lives, what question faces us for an answer?

in it the product of a "Master Architect," namely, God?

IS THERE A MASTER ARCHITECT WITH A PURPOSE?

⁵ Our viewpoint on the origin of things can have a far stronger influence on the way we look

at life, and on our attitude toward those around us, than many people realize. Uncertainty as to whether there is a universal Creator can make us uncertain about any definite purpose to life. It can also make us doubtful about what our true obligations are toward other humans. What happens then? Well, if we are unsure we just have to pattern our lives according to whatever each of us thinks best.

A watch has a maker . . .

That means our having no clear standard of right and wrong, no real sense of responsibility toward other people. It is not hard to see how many problems this could bring and how damaging it could be to the enjoyment of life.

⁶ What reason is there for believing in a Master

5. What effect can uncertainty or doubt as to whether there is a Creator have on our lives and on the lives of those around us?
6, 7. (a) Why do some people conclude there is no Creator, yet what may they be overlooking? (b) What conclusions as to a Creator might be logically drawn by comparing the universe to a watch? (Isaiah 40:26)

. . . What, then, of the awesome universe?

Architect, a God of purpose? Seeing so much injustice and suffering, some conclude that there is no Creator. But they may overlook the fact that there are many things that can be explained in no other way than by creation. If a person is shown a watch and told that the watch had no maker, he will not believe it, will he? He will probably acknowledge that this timekeeping instrument serves a definite purpose, which shows, additionally, that its maker had a purpose. What, then, will we say of the infinitely more complex and awesome universe around us? Perhaps the problem lies in not understanding what the Creator's purpose is. Let us consider a few evidences that a purposeful Creator *must* exist.

[7] The heavenly bodies have revolved in their vast orbits at tremendous speeds, with astounding precision, *for untold millions of years*. Planets orbit the sun in orderly fashion; the countless stars and other heavenly bodies are organized into galaxies and even clusters of galaxies. Their huge size and amazing accuracy of movement make the finest watch seem very crude by comparison. Are we not forced to ask ourselves, How could the watch have required a maker but not the far more awesome and precise universe? Further, could anything so intricate and accurate be without purpose?

[8] To say that all this precision and order came about through chance or blind forces would go against all the evidence. Do we know of anything orderly that ever came about by mere chance? No matter what we think of—a machine, a production line, a house or even a simple broom— each had a designer: man. Inanimate matter never arranges itself by chance into some orderly product or process. Regardless of how much time you allow, blowing winds or moving waters will never assemble matter to produce even the simplest machine. Everything that is made to serve a purpose requires an intelligent organizer and maker.

[9] Suppose we were to take the position that there is no Creator. Then we would be obliged to say that the universe has always existed, that the matter in it is eternal. Yet clear evidence shows that matter has not always existed. For example, we know that some elements of the earth are

---

8. Why is it contrary to the evidence to say that the universe is a product of chance or blind forces? (Hebrews 3:4)
9. How do radioactive materials provide evidence that matter has not *always* existed?

unstable, that is, they are radioactive. Uranium, for example, keeps giving off radioactive particles until it eventually turns into lead. But if matter had *always* existed there would be no radioactive elements left today. The radioactivity would have all 'run out' long ago, even as water eventually runs completely out of a leaking barrel.

[10] Another evidence is the different temperatures found in the universe, from the blazing heat of the sun to the frigid cold of outer space. The scientifically accepted laws as to the way heat operates (called the laws of thermodynamics) state that heat always flows from a hot body to a cooler one until both are at the same temperature. Now, if the universe and the matter in it had existed eternally, there would be (according to "thermodynamics") the same temperature everywhere, and a very cold one at that! But, thankfully, that is not the case. Our sun keeps on pouring out heat and energy, as do myriads of other stars. This proves that the universe, and the matter composing it, had a beginning.

[11] When scientists study matter, particularly the atom, they find evidence that all matter is the product of energy—enormous quantities of it. They once thought the atom was the simplest form of matter, the indivisible building block of all matter. But after years of study they find that the atom's structure is so complex that they are still unable to unlock all its secrets. Obviously, the source of tremendous energy that formed the atom, and all matter, and that set the universe in motion must be a *person*, with a mind far superior

10. How does the existence of different temperatures indicate that the universe had a beginning?
11, 12. To what conclusion does a study of the atom bring us?

to man's. Yes, these things are powerful, factual evidences that the universe did actually *originate* at some definite time in the past. It was *created*.

[12] And what about the planet we humans live on, this earth? What evidence of intelligent, purposeful design does its ability to sustain life reveal?

SUN AND EARTH—A PRECISE RELATIONSHIP

[13] Men have made atomic powerhouses—thermonuclear reactors—and their output of energy is greater than that by any other means. But they have to be monitored constantly for fear of a devastating explosion. Even so, some accidents have already happened. Now, the man-made reactors are puny, insignificant, compared to our sun. If the mighty, explosive processes in the sun were to go out of control, the earth could be burned up in an instant. Yet for billions of years, with apparently little or no change, the sun has steadily produced light and heat. It has been calculated that the conversion of only *one percent* of the sun's mass into energy would maintain its present intensity of light for at least a billion years.

[14] How reasonable is it, then, to conclude that man-made reactors required intelligent design, but that the vastly greater and far more dependable solar reactor, the sun, came into existence by mere chance? Should we not instead give the credit to a benevolent Master Architect for designing a solar "reactor" that safely transmits just the right amount of its enormous energy through some 93,000,000 miles (150,000,000 kilometers) of space to our earth?

13, 14. How does the sun give evidence of a powerful, benevolent Master Architect? (Psalm 74:16)

Man can hardly bear to look directly at the sun. Should he expect to gaze on its awesome Creator?

[15] Let us consider more closely the factors that make it possible for the earth to utilize the sun's energy in a way that ensures the continuance of life. Earth's distance from the sun is just right. If the sun were any closer the earth would be too hot for life; if farther away it would be too cold.

[16] Earth's rate of rotation provides the whole earth with alternate day and night periods of the proper length for plant growth. Plants, utilizing sun power, change water and carbon dioxide into sugars. This process, known as photosynthesis, is vital in producing food for animals and man. (Genesis 1:29, 30) The tilt of the earth's axis in

15. How is purposeful design shown in the earth's distance from the sun?
16. (a) What does the turning of the earth on its axis have to do with providing food for mankind and animals? (Psalm 104:14, 19-22) (b) What purpose is served, for our benefit, by the tilt of the earth's axis in its orbit around the sun? (Genesis 1:14; 8:22)

a fixed direction at an angle of about 23½ degrees from an upright position brings about the seasons. The time the earth takes for a trip around the sun makes the seasons just the proper length. While lengths of day and season vary somewhat in different parts of the earth, the abundant varieties of vegetation, nevertheless, get the required energy for growth.

OUR ATMOSPHERE—
IDEAL MEDIUM IN WHICH TO LIVE

[17] If any of the aforementioned features were significantly changed, it would mean disaster to life on earth. Yet they are only a fraction of the things essential for life. In fact, without an atmosphere surrounding our earth, the sun's light and energy would be useless, even dangerous. The earth's extensive atmosphere shields life from deadly rays. And the sun's radiation itself helps the atmosphere to produce a layer of ozone, a form of oxygen that filters out death-dealing ultraviolet rays.

[18] The makeup of earth's atmosphere is also very important if life is to continue. For example, we humans cannot live without oxygen. When deprived of it for just a few minutes, the brain is severely damaged. Usually death ensues. Is it not a very fine thing that oxygen exists in plentiful amounts in the atmosphere? But, then, oxygen is also what makes fire possible. So the vast quantity of this gas all around us could be destructive to life; we could be in danger of burning

17. How do the sun and the earth's atmosphere work together to provide protection from a deadly feature of the sun's radiation?
18. Does it just "happen" that there is plenty of oxygen in earth's atmosphere and that it is highly diluted with nitrogen? Explain.

up. Why does this not happen? Because the oxygen in our atmosphere is greatly diluted with nitrogen, a relatively inactive gas.

[19] Furthermore, the atmosphere has been prepared just as by a fine "recipe," with other essential ingredients in the right proportions—carbon dioxide, water vapor, and so forth. On the sun an atmosphere made up mainly of hydrogen is necessary, but in earth's atmosphere hydrogen, because of its explosive properties, would be a constant menace. Unless there is a Master Architect with a purpose, why would such a balance, a "cooperation," as it were, come about in the atmospheres of both sun and earth, so that the earth is so admirably fitted for life, while the sun, so far away, is equipped to sustain that life?

WATER—LIFE-SUSTAINING FLUID

[20] Besides an atmosphere with just the right

19. What conclusions may we reach from a comparison of the atmosphere of the sun with that of the earth?
20, 21. (a) Earth is unique among the planets in that it has great quantities of what vital substance? (b) What are some valuable purposes served by the mighty oceans?

How does it happen that on earth there is such an abundance of this liquid that is so essential for physical life?

mixture of gases, water in its normal liquid form
—lots of it—is essential for physical life. Of all
the planets, earth is unique in this respect. The
enormous volume of the oceans is the basis for
the rain cycle, which makes plant growth possible. The oceans also prevent extreme temperature fluctuation.

[21] Without the oceans another cycle—the oxygen and carbon-dioxide cycle—would fail. Oxygen
is used by animal life, carbon dioxide by plant
life. The oceans absorb and release billions of
tons of carbon dioxide as needed to keep the supply
balanced at all times. Of course, the oceans are
also a source of abundant mineral and animal
wealth.—Deuteronomy 33:19.

[22] Water is a unique, almost "miraculous" fluid.
It has the greatest solvent power of any liquid.
For this reason it can store the chemical compounds needed to support plant life. Water pene-
trates the soil and dissolves the life-sustaining
chemicals found there. It then carries these nu-
trients as it circulates to the various parts of the
plants. (Isaiah 55:10) Water is the primary con-
stituent of blood that carries life-giving nourishment to human and animal body cells. Our bodies
are, in fact, about 70 percent water.

[23] Remarkable, too, is the fact that water re-
mains liquid under a wide range of normal temperatures. If it evaporated faster, rain could not
stay on or in the ground to dissolve the minerals
and transport these to the plants. Vegetation
would lose its moisture too rapidly, and large
areas would become desert land. If the boiling

---

22. Why is water so valuable for the nourishment of plant and
animal life?
23. Why is water's stability as a liquid under a wide range of
temperatures important to our lives?

point of water were much lower than it is now, there would be the danger that our blood would boil when we were exposed to the hot sun. If water froze or solidified too readily, rainfall would be negligible and plants would die.

[24] Additionally, water expands slightly on becoming ice, therefore floating instead of sinking to the bottom. This prevents lakes and other large bodies of water from freezing solid, with consequent damage to life. This property of expansion plays a part in soil making, for water runs into cracks and crevices in rocks, then expands as it freezes, breaking the rocks into fine, tillable soil —all of this without man having to be concerned about it.

[25] How does it happen that, of all liquids, there is so much of this valuable water on earth? Surely it did not just happen. Its provision must be the work of a Master Architect—one who really cares for his living creation on earth!

THE EVIDENCE IS UNMISTAKABLE

[26] Truly, the person who takes a penetrating look at the visible evidence around him can see that there must be a supremely intelligent Personality, a Master Designer and Creator. Though this benevolent Designer cannot be seen with natural eyes, "his invisible qualities are clearly seen from the world's creation onward, because they are perceived by the things made, even his eternal power and Godship."—Romans 1:20.

---

24. What purposes are served by water's unusual property of expansion when freezing?
25. If we reason on the fact that the earth has such an abundant supply of water, what conclusion are we moved to reach? (Jeremiah 10:12, 13)
26. Though God is invisible to human eyes, how can we know that such a Master Designer and Creator exists?

[27] Some demand to *see* God before they will believe that he exists. But does it make sense to expect to see the One who created all these marvelous things? We can hardly bear to look directly at the sun, and certainly would be blinded and burned up if some of the larger suns were as close to earth as ours is. Then, what brilliance the Creator of these suns would display if he should reveal himself to human eyes! To Moses, who asked to see His glory, God replied: "You are not able to see my face, because no man may see me and yet live."—Exodus 33:20.

[28] However, if we use our powers of reason, we can see, in creation, an expression of unlimited power and control. Chance or blind forces cannot exercise purposeful control, or establish any laws. Law and control are evidences of the invisible qualities of a Master Architect. Also, the care with which the universe (including our solar system and planet earth) is put together, providing every good thing for the life of humankind, indicates great love and great concern. These are traits that can belong only to an intelligent and compassionate personality.

[29] But does God care for his creation in our day? Having designed and brought forth the universe, does he have further interest in dealing with it? Is there, in the mind of God, a future for man and a purpose toward every person who lives, or has lived?

---

27. Why is it not reasonable that we should demand to see God to believe that he exists?
28. In harmony with Romans 1:20, how can we see evidences of a Master Architect of love and care as we observe the universe?
29. Having concluded that there is a Creator, what questions deserve our next consideration?

Chapter 2

God
—The Generous Householder

SUPPOSE that you are traveling, looking for a suitable place to spend a vacation. After going a considerable distance in an isolated region, you come across a beautiful garden. You see a house and approach it to ask about accommodations. To your surprise a sign on the door reads: 'Welcome. Make yourself at home'! On entering the house, you find that it has everything desirable for comfortable living—water, heating, lights, plus a well-stocked pantry with a sign, 'Help yourself.' What would your reaction be? Would you say, 'This is unbelievable! What a kind, generous person the owner of this house must be!'?

2 Really, this illustration fits man's position in relationship to the Maker of the earth, God. Consider how the Creator, like a generous householder, has provided for those who have come to inhabit this planetary "home," the earth:

3 A fine home has a light, usually in the ceiling, and a soft night-light so that its inhabitants are not in utter darkness all night. The earth has the sun for its primary light source, and the soft light of the moon to 'dominate the night.'—Genesis 1:14-18.

4 A house has a power source for heating, operating appliances, and so forth. Earth has the sun. Not only does the sun bathe earth with energy that

1, 2. Considering our fine dwelling place, the earth, what would be our normal reaction, as "guests" on this planet?
3, 4. How is our fine "home" equipped for light, heat and power?

can be harnessed by man and by plant life, but its action over the centuries has provided an enormous supply of fuel, particularly fossil fuels such as coal and oil. These are stored, just as in a well-provisioned home, in earth's "cellar" for use when needed.

⁵ In this "cellar" the Creator also kindly placed a rich store of metals, and he gave man the ability to find ways of extracting these from the ores. For the special delight of men and, particularly, of women, He also placed in this "cellar" precious jewels that add to the joy of living, as well as chemicals that are essential to life.

⁶ A house also needs a good plumbing system. The "plumbing system" of our earthly "house" is a marvel. If man could build a mountain by amassing a great pile of rocks and dirt, would people living on it be able to get clear, cold, refreshing water out of springs on its slopes? We have seen huge man-made heaps in the vicinity of mines, and they are only unsightly blots upon the landscape. Consider, then, the marvelous engineering principles involved in the intricate system of channels and underground pressures by which the earth, even in the high mountains, has a water supply. And where there is little or no rain, such as in the Sahara Desert, there are places where it is necessary to dig only a relatively few feet to find water.

⁷ As in many fine homes where the floors are covered for beauty and comfort, the Creator also "carpeted" the earth with vegetation, flowers and forests. And with only a little landscaping, how quickly a desolate place can be made into a park! Places marred by man's activities soon are covered with a grass "carpet." Polluted streams, if the source of the pollution is stopped, soon cleanse themselves.

5. What other things for our comfort and delight are stored in the "cellar" of our "house"? (Job 28:1-6)
6. (a) How does the "plumbing system" of our planetary "home" give evidence of a Creator who cares for us? (b) Compare God's hills and mountains with man-made heaps of rock and dirt. (Psalm 104:10, 11)
7. How has the Creator provided a self-repairing "carpet" for our "home"? (Genesis 1:11, 12)

⁸ Just as a good home has a well-stocked pantry, in earth's "pantry" there is every form of food, in the fields and orchards, and in the oceans. Ponder over the wisdom that was needed to arrange, in advance, for vegetation in the sea and on land, for grains, and for fruit and nut trees to produce regularly, bountifully, for thousands and thousands of years, so that animals, insects, sea life and finally human life could all continue in existence. The supply never runs out. And earth can produce plentifully to feed yet many more, until God declares it to be 'filled' to a comfortable limit.—Genesis 1:28.

⁹ Surely none of us had anything to do with making this fine "house." The Bible tells us that to God "the heavens belong, but the earth he has given to the sons of men." (Psalm 115:16) The way our home, the earth, is equipped with everything needed for the enjoyment of life shows thoughtful preparation. And it is given to us free! What more convincing evidence could we want as testimony to the existence of a Maker who is not only powerful and wise but also kind and generous? He has, in effect, said to all, 'Help yourself,' letting "his sun rise upon *wicked people and good* and [making] it rain upon *righteous people and unrighteous.*" (Matthew 5:45) Really, if it were not for man's mismanagement and misuse of the earth's potential and resources, people in all lands could find real pleasure in living on this beautiful planet.

¹⁰ The fact that the earth, with little attention from man, has supplied his every need for cen-

---

8. What foresight and care were shown by our generous "Householder" in stocking the "pantry" of our "home"?
9. Can mankind take credit for his beautiful "home" and its equipment? (Job 38:4, 26, 27)
10. In view of the foregoing discussion, what can be said of the theory that the earth came to be as a result of blind forces?

turies, calls into serious question the theory that it came into existence as a result of blind forces. If a person accepted that theory, how could he explain earth's potential to provide for all its population, animal and human, millennium after millennium? Moreover, *purpose* and *design* are evident here. Blind forces are not capable of either purpose or preconceived design.—Jeremiah 10:12.

[11] The excellence of our earthly home certainly is convincing evidence that it was *created*, yes, more than this, that it was created for a definite purpose and is not just an experiment or a toy in the hands of some superior being. It is also designed to exist *forever*. "[The earth] will not be made to totter to time indefinite, or forever," says the inspired psalmist.—Psalm 104:5.

[12] What the Bible says about the preparation

11. What factors indicate that the earthly creation is not a mere experiment—a temporary thing or toy in the Creator's hands? (Isaiah 45:18)
12, 13. What pronouncement of God shows that no improvement on the earthly creation was needed?

As a well-provisioned home bespeaks a wise and generous householder . . .

of the earth as a home for man is in full harmony with this conclusion as to God's purpose for it. We learn that, as God completed the primary steps in the formation and preparation of the earth, he pronounced his creation "good." At the complete end of the work he declared it to be "very good." (Genesis 1:4, 10, 12, 18, 21, 25, 31) This divine pronouncement means that the work was perfect and fully adequate for its purpose—having an excellence beyond the power of im-

. . . so, too, the productive earth reveals intelligent design by a generous Creator

perfect man to comprehend.—Psalm 145:3-5, 16.

¹³ The earthly creation being declared "very good" also means that God does not need to intervene periodically to ensure that the earth will produce the necessary things for mankind. No, thousands upon thousands of years ago he spent much time in preparing and equipping this planet to fulfill its assigned role into the indefinite future. That fact magnifies the wisdom of the Creator. In what way?

GOD'S FORESIGHT

¹⁴ Well, think what insight, yes, foresight, it took on God's part to arrange for the earth to continue supporting life indefinitely. Before man came upon the scene, full provision was made for animal life, an ample supply of food being available in the form of vegetation. Then, the first human pair were told to "become many and fill the earth." (Genesis 1:28) This meant that the population of the human race would grow into the billions. Still the earth would continue to sustain plant, animal and human life. And it has done so despite the fact that millions of acres of land lie uncultivated and men have done much to ruin still other areas. Regarding the grand way in which God has provided, the appreciative psalmist wrote:

¹⁵ "[Jehovah] is making green grass sprout for the beasts, and vegetation for the service of mankind, to cause food to go forth from the earth, and wine that makes the heart of mortal man rejoice, to make the face shine with oil, and bread that

14, 15. How was extraordinary foresight shown by God at the time the earth was created?

sustains the very heart of mortal man. How many your works are, O Jehovah! All of them in wisdom you have made. The earth is full of your productions."—Psalm 104:14, 15, 24.

[16] How great is the ability of the earth to produce food? The director of the United Nations Office of Inter-Agency Affairs and Coordination said that, if earth's agricultural potential were maximized, it could feed at least 38 billion people (ten times earth's present population). This would, of course, require better international cooperation than now exists.

GOD WILL EXPEL "GUESTS"
WHO MISUSE HIS "HOUSE"

[17] Humankind in general has no room for complaint, but, rather, should appreciate the bounties of earth. Neither can they charge that God has been partial. Even those who do not worship him have benefited from his generosity. The apostle Paul told a group of people in Lystra, in Asia Minor, worshipers of Zeus and Hermes (Mercury): "In the past generations [God] permitted all the nations to go on in their ways, although, indeed, he did not leave himself without witness in that he did good, giving you rains from heaven and fruitful seasons, filling your hearts to the full with food and good cheer."—Acts 14:16, 17.

[18] But humans have been, generally, unthankful

16. Need we fear that earth will at some time fail to produce food sufficient for all? (Psalm 65:9)
17. Does anyone have reason to charge God with favoring only certain ones, such as his worshipers, with material abundance? (Psalm 36:7, 8)
18. (a) Have humans in general thanked or credited God for his goodness to all? (b) Who is to blame for the fact that there has been an inequality in the distribution of the good things God has provided?

"guests" of the Creator. They have to a great extent been disrespectful and wasteful of earth's fine provisions. Greed has caused hoarding of land and food. Such greedy persons have shown little care for their fellow "guests" on earth. As a result, many people have been deprived of the necessary things. Greed has been the basis for cruel, devastating wars.—Compare James 4:1, 2.

[19] With such a situation, there is a question as to whether our earthly "house" can ever be set in order. *From a human standpoint* it is impossible. As King Solomon said: "That which is made crooked cannot be made straight, and that which is wanting cannot possibly be counted." (Ecclesiastes 1:15) But God, as a good householder, is interested in his "house" and the "guests" in it. Would not a sensible householder throw out those who damaged the property, and clean up his house for the benefit of guests who will appreciate it? Should we not expect God to do the same? —Revelation 11:18.

[20] How will the Creator clean up the earth, misused for centuries? Does he purpose to keep it clean? Is it possible for earth to become a permanent paradise-like 'garden home' for man?

19, 20. (a) Can man hope to set matters straight in the earth for the good of all? (b) What is it reasonable that God, as a sensible householder, should do?

Chapter 3

A Paradise Home Ahead

MORE and more the complaint is being heard throughout the world that 'man is turning the earth into a vast garbage dump.' Is that actually going to happen?

² In spite of all the damage caused by human greed and violence, this planet is still filled with beauty—lush valleys, snowcapped mountains, plunging waterfalls, palm-lined beaches and a grand variety of plant and animal life. Are we to imagine that the Maker of all of this will permit mankind to mismanage and misuse earth's resources until this splendid planet becomes a lifeless sphere? Sound reasoning says No. What, then, does God have in mind for our earth? The material, visible, created things may tell us something about earth's Maker but they cannot tell us all we need to know. They cannot tell us what God's purposes are for the future. What, or who, then, can tell us?

³ In order to know, we need some revelation from the Maker himself. So that humans need not be in darkness regarding his purpose, the Almighty God, Jehovah, has provided a revelation in written form. It is found in the Bible. True, men wrote that book. But they acknowl-

---

1-3. (a) Why is it not reasonable to suppose that man will be allowed to abuse the earth until it becomes a lifeless sphere? (b) Can man, by observing creation and by his own reasoning, discover why things are as they are, and what God's purpose is? (Job 28:12-14, 28) (c) Where can we go to get an understanding of God and his purpose? (d) Is it reasonable to believe that God gave the Bible as a record of his thoughts and ways?

edged that what they recorded was not their own wisdom. One of the Bible writers, King David, declared: "The spirit of Jehovah it was that spoke by me, and his word was upon my tongue." (2 Samuel 23:2) Surely it was no difficult thing for the Designer of the human brain to activate the mental processes of men in a way that enabled them to write down His thoughts. The Bible being the only ancient book even making the claim of having been inspired by earth's Creator, Jehovah God, no other source can give us any idea about what he has in mind for the earth and man upon it.—2 Timothy 3:16, 17.

JESUS' PROMISE OF PARADISE

⁴ Words stated over nineteen centuries ago by an inspired man to a criminal clearly point to a grand future. That inspired man was Jesus, who is widely recognized as a prophet and one of the greatest teachers that ever lived. The Bible identifies him as the promised Messiah or Christ, the Son of God, who existed as a spirit person before his being born a human. (Matthew 16:13-16; Luke 1:30-33; Philippians 2:5-7) To the evildoer Jesus Christ said: "You will be with me in Paradise."—Luke 23:43.

⁵ This promise of Jesus Christ has been variously understood by Bible readers. Many Bible translations quote Jesus as saying: "Truly, I say to you, today you will be with me in Paradise." (*Common Bible*) In view of the punctuation, a

---

4. What outstanding man pointed to a grand future for humankind, and why should his words be believed?
5, 6. (a) What has caused Jesus' words at Luke 23:43 to be understood differently by various persons? (b) What gives us guidance as to how Jesus' words to the evildoer are to be understood?

person might conclude that the evildoer would be with Jesus in a paradise that very day. It should be noted, however, that little or no punctuation appears in the original Greek text. This makes it necessary for the translator to choose the placement of punctuation. Hence the words may also be punctuated to read: 'Truly I say to you today, you will be with me in Paradise.' The thought thus conveyed points to the evildoer's being with Jesus in Paradise at some future time.

⁶ This understanding of Jesus' words harmonizes with the rest of the Bible. That day, upon dying, Jesus did not go to heaven or to some intermediate place. He was dead in Hades,* gravedom, for three days (or parts thereof).—Matthew 27:62-66; Acts 2:24, 27.

⁷ Moreover, the evildoer would have understood Jesus' reference to "paradise" in harmony with the then current usage. And what was that?

---

* For a full discussion of this word *Hades*, along with the corresponding Hebrew word *Sheol*, see the book *Is This Life All There Is?*, published by Watchtower Bible and Tract Society of New York, Inc., 117 Adams Street, Brooklyn, New York 11201.

---

7. (a) How did the people understand the word "paradise" at the time Jesus Christ made his promise to the evildoer? (b) How can we prove that the man to whom Jesus spoke had no idea of going to a heavenly paradise?

committed and he was saying Jesus
remember me whenever
you might come into the kingdom of you and he said to
him Amen to you I am saying today, with me you will be
in the paradise and

Greek text of Luke 23:42, 43 from Vatican MS. 1209, with literal rendering, line for line, at the right

A paradise was a garden or park. The man was not a disciple of Jesus and so had no idea about a heavenly paradise. The books of the Bible available at that time did not hold forth to believers the opportunity of living in the spirit realm with God. It was not until the coming of Jesus Christ that attention was drawn to the hope of life in the invisible heavens. (2 Timothy 1:10) Though Jesus' disciples heard him talking about the "kingdom of the heavens," even they did not grasp fully just what was meant. (Matthew 13:24, 31, 33) Later, they asked the resurrected Jesus Christ: "Lord, are you restoring the kingdom to Israel at this time?" (Acts 1:6; compare the apostles' earlier words to Jesus at John 16:17, 18.) So they still thought in terms of the earth, expecting that Jesus would establish his kingdom in Jerusalem. Since Jesus' own disciples did not fully comprehend heavenly things at that time, how, then, could the evildoer possibly imagine that Jesus was speaking about something other than an earthly paradise?

[8] Jesus' promise to the evildoer is in agreement with statements in the Bible that the earth was made for a purpose. God "did not create it simply for nothing, [but] formed it even to be inhabited." (Isaiah 45:18; Psalm 104:5) It would be unreasonable to suppose that God, having spent centuries in preparing the earth with such care, would destroy it or leave it a waste just because some people did not appreciate it. Really, the

8. How was Jesus' promise to the evildoer in harmony with the Hebrew Scriptures, with which the Jews were generally acquainted?

earth itself has the potential for being a most delightful place to live.

PARADISE-LIKE "NEW EARTH" FORETOLD

[9] It is of note that the concept of an earthly paradise was long known to Jesus' fellow countrymen, the Israelites. When they moved into the Promised Land, it appeared to them as a paradise. Jehovah, through Moses, described it as far more beautiful and productive than even the rich Nile Valley where they had lived, saying:

[10] "For the land to which you are going to take possession of it is not like the land of Egypt out of which you came, where you used to sow your seed and you had to do irrigating with your foot, like a garden of vegetables. But the land to which you are crossing to take possession of it is a land of mountains and valley plains. Of the rain of the heavens it drinks water; a land that Jehovah your God is caring for. The eyes of Jehovah your God are constantly upon it, from the beginning of the year to the close of the year."—Deuteronomy 11: 10-12.

[11] In an earlier description of the land Moses had said:

"Jehovah your God is bringing you into a good land, a land of torrent valleys of water, springs and watery deeps issuing forth in the valley plain and in the mountainous region, a land of wheat and barley and vines and figs and pomegranates, a land of oil olives and honey, a land in which you will not eat bread with scarcity, in which you will lack nothing, a land the stones of which are iron and out of the mountains of which you will mine copper."—Deuteronomy 8:7-9.

9-11. (a) Had the Jews had any experience with what virtually amounted to an earthly paradise? When? (b) How did Moses describe the land of Palestine as a delightful place to live?

[12] Through his prophet Isaiah, God foretold long in advance that the nation of Israel would be taken by their enemies into exile for disobedience. Then their formerly paradise-like land would become desolate. But with this prophecy God did not leave the nation without hope, for he said: "I am creating new heavens and a new earth; . . . I am creating Jerusalem a cause for joyfulness and her people a cause for exultation." (Isaiah 65:17, 18) Here God was promising the restoration of Israel to the land of Judah, with Jerusalem again as capital. The "new heavens" would be, not new invisible heavens, but a *governorship* of the land of Judah in the hands of Zerubbabel of the tribe of Judah, a *rulership* over the land. The "new earth" was a repentant, cleansed, disciplined *people* brought back to their desolated land, which they began to cultivate and to beautify. They restored the worship of Jehovah God there and rebuilt the temple at Jerusalem.—Ezra 3:1, 2, 10.

[13] In their efforts to beautify the land of Judah to its former paradise-like state the Israelites received direct help from God, as indicated by Isaiah's prophecy about their return. God promised: "The wilderness and the waterless region will exult, and the desert plain will be joyful and blossom as the saffron." (Isaiah 35:1, 2) Similarly, the psalmist said that, when the nation would be obedient to God, "Jehovah, for his part, will give what is good, and our own land will give its yield."—Psalm 85:12.

---

12. When the nation of Israel returned from exile, how did God provide there in the land of Judah "new heavens" and a "new earth"?
13. What shows that God helped the restored Israelites in their efforts to bring about a paradise condition in their desolated land?

GLORIOUS "NEW EARTH" AHEAD

[14] Does this prophecy about a "new earth" have anything to do with us today? Yes, it is a glimpse of what God will do for the whole earth. Centuries after Isaiah prophesied, the apostle Peter wrote to Christians scattered over the then-known earth, saying: "There are new heavens and a new earth that we are awaiting according to his promise, and in these righteousness is to dwell." (2 Peter 3:13) This coming "new earth" society will therefore occupy a far larger area than that of ancient Judah.

[15] Moreover, the vision of the apostle John, recorded in the Bible book of Revelation, leaves no doubt that, in final fulfillment, the "new earth" society will inhabit the entire globe. The apostle John writes: "I saw a new heaven and a new earth; . . . 'Look! The tent of God is with *mankind,* and he will reside with them, and they will be his peoples.'" (Revelation 21:1-3) The expression "new heavens" has reference to God's rule from heaven where his throne is located. (Matthew 5:34) In due time, mankind will practice the true worship of God exclusively, and God's favor, help and protection will be with them. The "new heavens" will extend blessings to humankind on a beautified earth.—Psalm 115:16.

[16] That this fine destiny for the earth is what God purposes is shown by his dealings with the human race. According to the Bible, the first

14. What assurance do we have that the prophecies about the "new earth" have even greater meaning to us today?
15. What does the vision given to the apostle John reveal to us about the coming earthly paradise?
16, 17. (a) How does the book of Genesis show that God's original purpose for man was everlasting life in a paradise? (b) How does God's prophecy at Genesis 3:15 reveal that God did not abandon his purpose when Adam sinned?

man, Adam, was told that it would be only for disobedience that he would die. Therefore, if he had remained obedient, he would never have died. (Genesis 2:17; 3:19) He would have continued to live and the paradise garden would have continued as the God-given home of perfect man. As Adam's family grew they would gradually have spread the paradise into the land outside, under God's direction.

[17] After Adam's sin, God gave indication to Adam's offspring that he had not abandoned his purpose toward the earth. He promised to bring forth a "seed," an offspring who would be a liberator of mankind. (Genesis 3:15) Having this purpose toward the human race, God let Adam have children. They could live with this promise as their hope.

[18] Later, this hope of a future paradise was strengthened by the revelation to Abraham that the "seed" would come through his line of descent

and would *bless all families of the earth.*' (Genesis 22: 18) About eight hundred years farther down the stream of time, God told King David of Jerusalem that his offspring would sit on the throne forever. (2 Samuel 7:12, 13, 16) Everything pointed to *one*

18. (a) What later revelation showed that the promise of the "seed" would be of importance to mankind right here on earth? (b) Who would be the "seed," and what authority would he have?

Men of faith looked forward to a government of God, in heaven, that would rule the earth

son of David's line, superior to all previous kings of that line. This would be the Messiah (meaning "anointed one") who would occupy the throne of David forever. (Psalm 45:6, 7; Galatians 3:16) The apostle Paul applies this prophecy to Jesus Christ, the Son of God, born on earth in the line of David. Paul says of him: "God is your throne forever," that is, God is the foundation and support of Christ's throne for all time to come. —Hebrews 1:8, 9.

[19] Throughout the Psalms, written over a period of centuries, reference is repeatedly made to God's righteous rule over earth "to time indefinite" and "to time indefinite, even forever." (Psalms 9:7, 8; 10:16, 17; 29:10; 145:21) All these prophecies find fulfillment in the rulership of Jesus Christ,

19. How do the Psalms make it sure to us that the paradise brought about through Christ the "seed" will endure forever?

God will clean out of the earth all who do harm

whom God raised from the dead and exalted to the highest position next to himself. (Ephesians 1:20-22) That men will live forever in this paradise home, Psalm 37:29 reveals by declaring: "The righteous themselves will possess the earth, and they will reside forever upon it."

BEFORE PARADISE, A CLEANSED EARTH

20 But the question arises, Just how will God ensure that there will be permanent peace on earth, so that the enjoyment of living will not be marred? Just as a man would begin the cleaning up of his house by ousting bad tenants, God purposes to make way for permanent peace on a renewed earth by cleansing it of bad elements. He did this for ancient Israel when he drove out the corrupt Canaanite nations who had been in possession of the land so that Israel could possess it in peace.—Leviticus 18:24-27.

21 Today, many people would like to see peace

20. What example do we have to assure us that God will remove from the earth all elements that would be destructive of peace?
21. Why, at the present time, is it impossible to have altogether righteous conditions, even though many people have that desire?

and righteousness on earth. But the present system of things—dominated by powerful religious, political and commercial elements—has the people in a viselike grip. It is hard for people to do what is right. And the good news of God's purpose toward the earth is opposed by the clergymen of the dominant religious systems, by growing atheism and by the news and propaganda channels. The Bible says that the nations walk "in the unprofitableness of their minds, while they are in darkness mentally, and alienated from the life that belongs to God, because of the ig-

In a cleansed earth there will be enduring happiness

norance that is in them, because of the insensibility of their hearts."—Ephesians 4:17, 18; compare John 3:19.

²² This system of things has covered the earth, as it were, with a blinding veil. But God promises to tear away that veil. Prophetically he said that he would destroy "the covering that is cast over all peoples, the veil that is spread over all nations." —Isaiah 25:7, *Revised Standard Version*.

²³ Jesus Christ, as heavenly King, will bring about the end of this system of things in what is called in the Bible "the war of the great day of God the Almighty." (Revelation 16:14) Those persons seeking to do what is right need not fear that war, for it will be selective, getting rid of those who do harm to their fellowman and who do not want to serve God. Through their selfishness and greed these wicked ones are "ruining the earth," hence they themselves must be brought to ruin.—Revelation 11:18; 2 Peter 2:9.

²⁴ So God promises to do away with the system of things that oppresses people. Along with this, God purposes also to clean out those who persist in misleading, defrauding and oppressing their fellowman. (Psalms 72:4; 103:6) As long as such "tenants" remain in God's earthly "house" there cannot be peace and happiness for those who sincerely want it. There is no other way. The *price* of a paradise is the removal of these greedy ones. The rule is: "The wicked is a ransom for

22. What does God promise to do in behalf of those who want to do what is right?
23. (a) Why does a war have to be fought to clean up the earth? (b) Who do not need to fear that war, and why not?
24. Why is there no other way to bring peace and happiness than by removing those greedy persons who persist in opposing their fellowman?

the righteous one." Says the proverb: "The righteous is the one rescued even from distress, and the wicked one comes in instead of him." That is, the wicked one, who has been causing distress, receives retribution, bringing relief from distress for the righteous one.—Proverbs 21:18; 11:8.

25 This cleaning out of the present world system in which false religion, politics, commerce and materialism dominate will remove injustice and oppression. The Bible likens the agency used to a great windstorm: "Look! The windstorm of Jehovah, rage itself, will certainly go forth, even a whirling tempest. Upon the head of the wicked ones it will whirl itself. The anger of Jehovah will not turn back until he will have carried out and until he will have made the ideas of his heart come true. In the final part of the days you people will give your consideration to it with understanding."—Jeremiah 23:19, 20.

26 God's rule will then be undisputed in the earth. But will it bring in permanent happiness, without a reverting to disobedience and the ruin of paradise at a later time? The reason why its operation will be vastly superior to man-rule is a topic that deserves our attention next.

25, 26. (a) To what does the Bible liken the cleanup of the earth? (b) What question arises as to the permanence of the cleansed earth?

Chapter 4

Do We Need Rulership by God?

WHEN you look around and see the many undesirable things going on all over the earth—sickness, injustice, crime, hatred and war —you may find it difficult to harmonize this with the idea that there is a supreme power governing the universe.

[2] You might say, 'If I were the Creator, I would do something about it now.' Many people show that they feel this way when they ask, 'Why doesn't God do something? Does God care?'

[3] But, assuming that you were powerful enough to put an immediate stop to all things causing trouble, would this make people happy? It would require you to make sweeping changes in all the systems and institutions of this world, in fact, a total change in the way that the world operates. It would demand drastic alterations in everyone's personal plans and ways of life. Would these forcible changes meet with a warm welcome by everyone? Hardly. People do not want to be forced into a way of life. As they say, they 'want to do their own thing.'

FREEDOM OF WILL ESSENTIAL

[4] For people to get along together in happiness

1, 2. What may a person think when he sees the bad conditions in the earth?
3. If a man had the power to make forcible changes in this world, could he make people happy?
4, 5. Are people happy if their lives are regulated in all things? Give an example.

a change of mind and heart is needed. This change cannot be brought about through the mere exercise of power and authority. People must be *willing* to change.

⁵ For example, a man may be a loving father providing the necessities of life, along with some extras, for his son or daughter. But what if the father uses his authority to regulate every detail of the child's life, even when the child becomes grown? True, the child may have an apparently secure life with no material needs. But will he (or she) be happy? No. Often we hear the complaint made by children of rich and powerful men: 'I want to live my own life. I prefer to make my own decisions. I may make some mistakes but at least my life would be real.' Such persons thus show they actually feel insecure, in spite of all their apparent advantages. Total domination does not lead to human happiness.

⁶ God, who made mankind, knows that humans have this deep-rooted feeling. He made them "in

6. Why, basically, do people want freedom to do as they see fit?

A good father reasons with his son, realizing that the boy must make decisions. So God acknowledges the free will of his intelligent creatures

his image," which includes having a generous
measure of free will and choice. (Genesis 1:27)
God could have made humans like automatons,
constructed so that they could do no wrong. But
he did not. Neither are they directed by built-in
instinct, as are animals. God made men with
their own free will and the desire to exercise it.

⁷ As a result, mankind cherishes freedom, sometimes more than life itself. However, so that every
human can take a wise course in his exercise of
free will, God has provided guidance in the form
of a conscience and, in addition, His own wise
counsel and instructions. But God is not dictatorial.
He does not force people into the course of action
that he recommends. For this wise manner of
dealing with us we should be really grateful.
—Romans 2:4; 2 Peter 3:15.

⁸ Many people feel that admitting God's existence and acknowledging his rule would be sure
to conflict with their exercise of free will. Therefore they prefer human rulership, even though
human rule brings its own restrictions, even hardships. They choose to tolerate man-rule rather
than to seek God's rulership. Why? Because man-
rule allows for a considerable measure of selfishness. It does not demand deep-seated internal
changes—a making over of one's personality.
Man-rule does not require the bringing of one's
life into line with what is wholly right, as God's
rule encourages. If a person doubts this, all he
needs to do is to look about to see whether he
finds real love of neighbor and a following of

7. (a) What factor has God provided so that people can exercise their free will wisely? (b) What qualities has Jehovah God
displayed in not forcing men to obey him, as pointed out at
Romans 2:4 and 2 Peter 3:15?
8. Why do many people prefer man-rule to God's rule?

clean, honest, upright principles in the everyday lives of the majority of mankind.

[9] However, even under man-rule, people have never been really content. And today people are getting more and more dissatisfied with all man-made forms of rule. This is evidenced by the many public demonstrations against certain governmental policies. It is manifested even more strongly in the internal upheavals, revolutions and changes in government around the world. Yet many people do not think of rulership by God as the way to genuine relief. Why?

IS GOD "DEAD"?

[10] Some say, "God is dead," that is, he is uninterested in man's affairs and is indifferent, with no intention of asserting his authority. Never is this so! The amazing care, even to the smallest detail, that God displayed in forming the universe shows that he has intense interest in his creations and particularly in man 'made in his image.'

[11] When on earth his Son taught that believers should pray to God: "Let your kingdom come. Let your will take place, as in heaven, also upon earth." (Matthew 6:10) He urged people to look to a time when God would exercise undisputed rulership over the earth. God himself spoke to some who doubted his interest in them and who questioned his "aliveness." He made it clear to them by words and actions that "Jehovah is alive

---

9. Though most people have chosen rulership by man, what does the evidence show as to whether they are happy and satisfied?
10. What do persons mean who say "God is dead," and what is one strong evidence that they are not correct?
11. How do the words of Jesus Christ and of Jehovah himself show that God is interested in man's affairs?

in truth, in justice and in righteousness!"
—Jeremiah 4:2.

¹² Well, then, is God waiting for men to abandon
man-rule and ask him to be their sole ruler? No.
The nations will never willingly give their rulership over to God. The Bible prophetically says:
"Why have the nations been in tumult and the
national groups themselves kept muttering an
empty thing? The kings of earth take their stand
and high officials themselves have massed together
as one against Jehovah and against his anointed
one [or, Christ], saying: 'Let us tear their bands
apart and cast their cords [all requirements and
restrictions that God's rule would bring] away
from us!' "—Psalm 2:1-3.

¹³ Jehovah declares: "I am the Alpha and the
Omega, the first and the last, the beginning and
the end." (Revelation 22:13) Since Alpha and
Omega are the first and last letters of the Greek
alphabet, God means that when he begins a thing,
he *sees it through to its conclusion.* Moreover,
Bible history gives account after account in which
God took a hand in the affairs of men. These acts
manifested his keen interest in accomplishing
what he wanted at the time. They were all steps
toward fulfilling his purpose that his will be done
on earth in his appointed time, as will be discussed
later.

¹⁴ Why is God's rulership the one that we need?
Because the rule of earth that can bring peace
and harmony cannot come from any other source.

---

12. Why is God not waiting for humankind to ask him to rule
over them?
13. (a) What does God mean when he says: "I am the Alpha
and the Omega"? (b) Do we have evidence of God's inter-
vention in the affairs of humankind?
14. How can we be sure that man-rule can never bring peace
and happiness to earth?

No person or body of persons among men and women can exercise proper rule over humankind. In making the earth, it was not God's purpose to have humans rule mankind. When the Israelites demanded a king like the other nations, God made it clear to them that this would lead to problems, including the loss of freedom. This proved to be the case. (1 Samuel 8:7-9) Even one of Israel's kings, a man who devoted much time to a study of life and its problems, spoke of *'man dominating man to his injury.'*—Ecclesiastes 8:9.

[15] In the beginning, God gave man no authority to dominate or rule over other men. God told him to "be fruitful and become many and fill the earth and subdue it, and have in subjection *the fish of the sea and the flying creatures of the heavens and every living creature that is moving upon the earth.*" (Genesis 1:28) But men have gone beyond this and *assumed* domination over other men and have fought for it.

[16] God's wisdom in not giving men domination over one another can be seen by examining world history. As regards any *earthly* ruler, he may do well for a while, but the people's interests generally become more and more unimportant to him as his rule continues. The saying 'Power corrupts' is true, because in time a human ruler comes to take undue advantage of his authority. He usually becomes partial, favoring persons he likes, particularly those from whom he receives things, and this to the hurt of others. Often, those close to him deceive him as to the facts and prevent

---

15. What was the extent of the dominion that God gave to man?
16, 17. (a) How is God's wisdom manifest in his not giving men rulership over other men? (b) How did God's inspired prophet express the reason why man is unable to rule over his fellowman?

others from approaching him. Some of these fear to bring the true state of affairs to his attention.

[17] Rulership over others is too much for any man. He gradually loses touch, not knowing what is going on at the "grass-roots" level of the common people. The Bible accounts show that the very best of human rulers made serious mistakes. It is as the prophet said: "I well know, O Jehovah, that to earthling man his way does not belong. It does not belong to man who is walking even to direct his step."—Jeremiah 10:23.

GOD'S RULERSHIP THE ONLY SATISFACTORY ONE

[18] Not so, however, with the Almighty God. It is evident from the wisdom manifest in the universal creation that his scope of understanding is great. (Psalm 147:5) He has complete knowledge of every detail of creation and of every law governing it. (Isaiah 40:12-14) Reasoning leads us to conclude that a supreme power upholds, sustains and controls the material universe. Would not such a ruler be one to whom it would be wise to submit?

[19] There is no partiality in the exercise of God's rulership, as is the case with earthly rulers. The opportunity to become his friend is open to all. He needs nothing from his creatures. He cannot be bribed. (Psalm 50:9-12) All are on the same level before him, for who can give the Creator anything? The apostle Paul asks: "Who has first given to him, so that it must be repaid to him?" —Romans 11:35.

---

18. Why is rulership by God the only satisfactory one?
19. In dealing with individuals, how is God outstandingly superior to human rulers?

From our birth God knows our traits and individual needs; he can provide the right kind of rulership for all mankind

[20] A proper ruler over humankind would have to know the human makeup through and through. Of no one but Jehovah can it be said: "You have become familiar even with all my ways. For there is not a word on my tongue, but, look! O Jehovah, you already know it all. Your eyes saw even the embryo of me, and in your book all its parts were down in writing, as regards the days when they were formed and there was not yet one among them."—Psalm 139:3, 4, 16.

[21] *God is concerned with and interested in every one of us.* "The eyes of Jehovah are in every place, keeping watch upon the bad ones and the good ones," says the inspired proverb. (Proverbs 15:3; compare 2 Chronicles 16:9; 1 Peter 3:12.) To what extent can we rely on his care? Jesus Christ said: "Do not two sparrows sell for a coin

20. Why is it only God as Ruler who can know what is altogether best for everyone?
21. Show that God takes an interest, not merely in people as a whole, but in each individual.

of small value? Yet not one of them will fall to the ground without your Father's knowledge. But the very hairs of your head are all numbered. Therefore have no fear: you are worth more than many sparrows." (Matthew 10:29-31) Only the Creator knows the minds and hearts of men. "As for Jehovah, he sees what the heart is." (1 Samuel 16:7) He alone knows what is needed to mold willing-hearted ones so that he can bring them into a state of unity and peace with him and with one another.

²² 'Why, then,' you may ask, 'does God let man exercise rulership? Why does He not assert His sovereign rule *now,* doing away with mankind's suffering, and establishing peace?' This he has certainly promised to do. But he has a time for it, no later, we can be sure, than is absolutely necessary. To those who thought God slow, the apostle Peter wrote: "Jehovah is not slow respecting his promise, as some people consider slowness, but he is patient with you because he does not desire any to be destroyed but desires all to attain to repentance."—2 Peter 3:9.

²³ Peter also counseled: "However, let this one fact not be escaping your notice, beloved ones, that one day is with Jehovah as a thousand years and a thousand years as one day." (2 Peter 3:8) Since Jehovah lives forever and is not bounded by time, he is different from humans, who have to accomplish their aims in a few short years. Because of his limitless scope of view of the past, present and future, he can act at the most appropriate time, the time that will result in salvation and life to the greatest number of people.

22, 23. What may be said in answer to the questions: 'Why does not God take over rulership of the earth now? Is he slow?'

And because of his power to resurrect the dead, any harm formerly done to them can be erased, reversed.—Luke 20:37, 38.

[24] Jehovah God as Ruler and Controller of the vast starry universe, in which the earth is a mere speck by comparison, is no less interested in this "speck." He is concerned in exercising complete sovereign rule over his intelligent creatures in heaven and on earth, and in seeing to their happiness. To rule over intelligent, living creatures, to have them willingly and knowingly submit to his sovereignty, is much more glorifying to God and the splendor of his rulership than having the unintelligent, inanimate stars obey him in their courses. This kind of intelligent harmony he purposes to restore. (Psalm 66:3, 4) And in accomplishing this, God will not do one thing more, or less, than is absolutely necessary.

[25] But what brought about disharmony and the need for God's action to restore peace to the earth? The answer to this question also helps in answering many others, such as: 'Why has wickedness been permitted?' 'Why over such a long time?' It is of *greatest importance* for us to get a correct and thorough understanding of this matter. Let us investigate it.

---

24. (a) Is God, as Ruler of the vast universe, unconcerned about this comparatively insignificant planet? (b) Why is it of greater honor to God to have people obey him than it is to have the stars and planets operating according to his will?
25. What is the important question that we should consider next?

Chapter 5

Why Has God Allowed Suffering on Earth?

SCIENTIFIC evidence and the Bible testify that all humans sprang from one original pair. Then, after the Flood, three main branches of the human family were formed from the offspring of the three sons of Noah.—Genesis 3:20; 9:18, 19.

² The apostle Paul said: "[God] made out of one man every nation of men, to dwell upon the entire surface of the earth." (Acts 17:26) This man Adam and his wife, Eve, were created perfect, as are all God's works.—Deuteronomy 32:4; Genesis 2:18, 21-23.

³ Adam was a *son of God,* a full-fledged member of God's family, made only a little lower than angels. (Luke 3:38) Angels are spirit creatures greater in power and ability than humans. (2 Peter 2:11) But nowhere does the Bible state that the angels have greater moral capacity. When Jesus Christ was on earth as a man, born of a woman, his moral integrity was equal to that of anyone in God's universal family in heaven and on earth. —Psalm 8:4, 5; Hebrews 2:6-9; 7:26.

⁴ How, then, did imperfection and its accompanying troubles, sickness and strife, come to be the lot of the human race? The Bible explains that,

1, 2. How did the human race get its start, and what kind of start was it?
3. How did Adam, at the time of his being created, compare with angels?
4, 5. How did sickness, trouble and suffering come upon the entire human race?

through no fault of their own, all humans since Adam and Eve have been born with imperfections. It declares: "Through one man sin entered into the world and death through sin, and thus death spread to all men because they had all sinned." —Romans 5:12.

[5] According to the laws of genetics, children inherit tendencies and characteristics, as well as defects, from their parents. But how did perfect Adam become defective, imperfect, a sinner? Why have trouble and suffering been allowed since then?

ADAM'S FINE POSITION

[6] Adam was created in God's image and likeness. (Genesis 1:26) This means that he had moral qualities and a capacity for spirituality. He could know and learn about God and could have a son-like relationship with God. He had reasoning powers and the faculty of conscience—a sense of right and wrong. Adam was able to represent God on earth, reflecting God's glory—his fine attributes—to those who would be born.

[7] God was in communication with Adam, possibly every day. According to Genesis 3:8, it was "about the breezy part of the day" that Adam and Eve "heard the voice of Jehovah God." The reference to a specific period during the day suggests that this may have been the customary time for God to communicate with man. Yes, the Most High did take time to teach Adam as a newcomer on earth. (Genesis 1:28-30) This first man needed God's help and instruction, so that he could come to exercise proper dominion

6. In what way was Adam created 'in God's image and likeness'?
7. (a) How did God provide for Adam's need as a newcomer on earth? (b) How should Adam have responded?

over the lower creation. Adam had full capacity
for spiritual development and for cultivating love.
He could become stronger in appreciation and
love for his Creator as he progressed in learning.
(1 John 4:7, 8) He could establish an ever closer
relationship with Him.

⁸ The Bible does not state how long a period
of time God occupied in giving his son instruction.
But it was essential that Adam learn, among the
first things, about plant life and animal life, since
he was to be the expert cultivator, and instructor
of his children in the art of gardening and caring
for domestic animals. (Genesis 2:15, 19) This
obviously could take some time.

⁹ Adam dwelt in the Edenic garden home that
God had made for him. It was likely a large area
around which Adam could travel. Thus, Adam
could observe the animals in their habitat, in
whatever way God would facilitate this. Adam
could then name them according to their traits
and characteristics. There was no need for haste.
—Genesis 2:8, 19, 20.

¹⁰ While Adam could solve problems that would
arise within the scope of his knowledge, he would
have to look to God as the Designer and Director
as to just how he was to 'subdue the earth.' The
uncultivated earth outside the garden of Eden
would have to be made "home" for billions of
persons to come. And just as a builder follows the
blueprints of the architect, so man would need to
follow God's wise direction faithfully in order to
fashion earth for beauty and for the greatest

8. Why was it essential that Adam learn much about plant and
animal life?
9. What assignment did God give Adam, according to Genesis
2:19, 20, and how was Adam able to carry it out properly?
10. With the training that Adam received, what would Adam
be able to do, but what care was he to exercise?

comfort and enjoyment to the human race.—Luke 16:10.

¹¹ How did Adam do as to the things with which God had blessed him? For a time he did well, instructing his wife just as he had learned

With instruction from God, Adam learned how to exercise dominion over the animals

from God. (Compare Genesis 2:16, 17 with Genesis 3:2, 3.) By reason of his Creatorship, Jehovah was their God. To continue in proper relationship to God, Adam and Eve needed to lean upon and obey him as Sovereign Ruler. As they would expand their family to cover the earth, subjection to God's rulership would be essential for order and harmony. Adam and Eve could teach and train their children, so that they, in turn, might bring glory to God.

'THE TREE OF KNOWLEDGE'

¹² God had told Adam that he could eat freely of every tree of the garden except for the tree of the knowledge of good and bad. (Genesis 2:17) Everlasting life was set before this couple and their offspring, conditioned only on their obe-

---

11. How did Adam carry out his responsibility at first, and what duties were ahead of him?
12. What prospect did Adam and Eve have, according to Genesis 2:17?

dience. It would be a disgrace upon God's entire family in heaven and on earth for Adam to be so disrespectful as to disobey God.

[13] God had given Adam everything for his enjoyment. Adam himself did not make the earth to produce the fine things to eat. He did not create his beautiful companion Eve. He did not make his own body, with the faculties that enabled him to enjoy the things he had. But, while Adam loved and enjoyed the fine life he had been kindly given, he did not follow through in an obedient way.

[14] Eventually Adam came to put his supposed interests above those of his heavenly Father. He thought more of his immediate desires than of the family of God and the offspring that he was to have. Even imperfect humans despise a man who is a traitor to his family and who sells his own children into slavery and death. And that is what Adam did.—Romans 7:14.

[15] Of what did Adam's sin consist? It was in connection with the "tree of the knowledge of good and bad." Much conjecture has been put forward about this tree. Was it a real tree? What was the "knowledge" and the "good and bad"? Why would God put such a tree in the garden?

[16] The Bible indicates that the tree was real, speaking of it as one among the fruit trees of the garden. (Genesis 2:9) What was the "knowledge" that the tree represented? The Catholic *Jerusalem Bible* makes a pertinent comment, in a footnote on Genesis 2:17:

13, 14. (a) Why was it entirely right and proper that Adam obey God? (b) What did Adam fail to do with respect to the good things he had, and what attitude did he develop?
15, 16. (a) Was the "tree of the knowledge of good and bad" a real tree? (b) What other questions arise concerning this tree?

[17] "This knowledge is a privilege which God reserves to himself and which man, by sinning, is to lay hands on, [Genesis] 3:5, 22. Hence it does not mean omniscience, which fallen man does not possess; nor is it moral discrimination, for unfallen man already had it and God could not refuse it to a rational being. It is the power of deciding for himself what is good and what is evil and of acting accordingly, a claim to complete moral independence by which man refuses to recognise his status as a created being. The first sin was an attack on God's sovereignty, a sin of pride."

[18] The tree was, in effect, symbolic of the boundary—the line of demarcation—or the limit of man's proper domain. It was right and proper, yes, essential, that God inform Adam of that boundary. For a perfect man to eat of that tree would require the deliberate assent of his will. It would indicate the determination made beforehand that he would withdraw himself from subjection to God's rulership, to go out on his own, doing what was "good" or "bad" according to his own decisions.

GOD'S SOVEREIGNTY CHALLENGED

[19] So man went in a way independent of God. God did not interfere with Adam's free will. But Adam's wrong choice brought him and his children into all kinds of troublesome, humanly unsolvable problems.—Romans 1:28.

[20] Moreover, there was more to the issue than the mere rebellion of Adam and his wife. The

---

17. According to a footnote in the Catholic *Jerusalem Bible,* what was the "knowledge" that the tree stood for?
18. (a) Of what was the tree symbolic? (b) For a perfect man to sin by eating of the 'tree of knowledge' what decision would he first make?
19. What did Adam's willful sin bring upon himself and his children, in harmony with the principle at Romans 1:28?
20. How did Adam's wrong act raise a question that included all mankind?

rebellion of the earthly son of God raised the question: Would anyone within God's earthly family, using his free will, choose to be loyal to God's rulership, and would any stay loyal to God under pressure, or under the temptation of gaining something for himself by disobedience? So the integrity, the faithfulness, of every man and woman to be brought into existence would be a matter of doubt in the minds of all God's creatures in heaven and on earth.

[21] This question was, however, subsidiary or secondary to a far greater one—a challenge regarding the *rightfulness of God's sovereignty or rulership*—as was illustrated by developments some 2,500 years later. An illustration of the issue involved is found in what happened in real life to the man Job, a record of which was preserved for our benefit.

[22] The book of Job reveals that a heavenly angel of God was the promoter of the challenge. He appeared before the Most High, insolently accusing God's devoted servant Job, saying that his loyalty to God was based solely on selfishness. God allowed this spirit son to bring a test of great adversity upon Job. Even though Job proved faithful under the test, the rebel still accused Job of having a bad heart. Jehovah said to him: "Have you set your heart upon my servant Job, that there is no one like him in the earth, a man blameless and upright, fearing God and turning aside from bad? Even yet he is holding fast his integrity [blamelessness, faithfulness to God], al-

---

21. The sin of Adam raised what issue far greater than the question of human integrity?
22. How does the book of Job show that the integrity and loyalty of every human were actually made a subject of controversy?

though you incite me against him to swallow him up without cause." The angel answered: "Skin in behalf of skin, and everything that a man has he will give in behalf of his soul. For a change, thrust out your hand, please, and touch as far as his bone and his flesh and see whether he will not curse you to your very face."—Job 2:2-5.

[23] God let Job be tested, knowing that he would remain faithful. And Job did not actually lose by suffering for a while. For, at the end of the test, God rewarded Job beyond anything he had formerly enjoyed, including 140 more years of life. —Job 42:12-16; compare Hebrews 11:6.

[24] This glimpse of an invisible heavenly occurrence helps us to see the real issue as to God's allowance of evil. The challenging angel, known as Satan the Devil, was actually the instigator of the rebellion. Nonetheless, the first human pair, who took the side of Satan when he first set the challenge in motion, were willfully at fault, without excuse.

[25] God had given Adam all the necessary instruction and opportunities to become fully equipped to stand loyally by God, for God would never leave a servant of His open to an attack for which he had no defense. (1 Corinthians 10:13) Consequently, Adam, being perfectly free to exercise his will, could have stood firm and demonstrated loyalty and faithfulness. There were no factors beyond his control to make him sin,

23. What was the result to Job for holding fast to faithfulness under severe suffering?
24. (a) Who, actually, was the instigator and promoter of the rebellion against God? (b) Were Adam and Eve therefore excusable?
25, 26. (a) Since it was Satan the Devil who attacked Adam as to his loyalty to God, did God unfairly leave Adam open to attack? (b) What may have been Satan's reasoning, as he set about to attack Eve?

as is the case with imperfect mankind today. His sin was entirely willful and deliberate.

[26] Nevertheless, God's adversary, the rebellious spirit son, sought an opportunity to initiate rebellion in the universe. He wanted to use Adam and Eve as instruments to promote his challenge of God's rulership. The Bible account tells us how he attacked the woman first. Satan had confidence that, having overcome Eve, he would be able to put great pressure upon Adam.

REBELLION AGAINST GOD

[27] How was the challenge to God's rulership, that Satan had in mind, actually set in motion? The Bible account reports that a lowly beast of the field, a serpent, spoke to Eve. Of course, an animal cannot speak of itself. Satan the Devil was actually the speaker, using the serpent. Because of this deception and the use of the serpent, God called him "the original serpent [deceiver]." (Revelation 12:9) Jesus pointed out that Satan was the instigator of the challenge to God's sovereignty when he said that the Devil was "the father of the lie" and a manslayer from the beginning of his rebellious course in Eden. (John 8:44) The Bible record of this first lie and the rebellion reads:

[28] "Now the serpent proved to be the most cautious of all the wild beasts of the field that Jehovah God had made. So it began to say to the woman: 'Is it really so that God said you must not eat from every tree of the garden?' At this the woman said

27. Though a serpent spoke to Eve, how do we know that the serpent was really only the instrument of the Devil?
28. From the account in Genesis 3:1-5: (a) How did Satan's question to Eve imply that God had held back something from her that she should have? (b) Was Eve ignorant of God's law about not eating from the 'tree of knowledge'?

to the serpent: 'Of the fruit of the trees of the garden we may eat. But as for eating of the fruit of the tree that is in the middle of the garden, God has said, "You must not eat from it, no, you must not touch it that you do not die."' At this the serpent said to the woman: 'You positively will not die. For God knows that in the very day of your eating from it your eyes are bound to be opened and you are bound to be like God, knowing good and bad.'"—Genesis 3:1-5.

²⁹ Previous to this time the woman had obeyed the injunction not to eat of the 'tree of knowledge' to which the serpent referred. She had all manner of food to eat and was in no need. She understood that to eat from the tree would bring bad results. Not that the fruit was poison, but God had said that eating it would bring his judgment of death. Now, if a person in the woods sees certain plants, such as poison ivy, or certain trees the fruit of which is dangerous to eat, is he attracted or impelled to touch, take and eat of them? No, there is no such attractiveness. This was the way with Eve. But Satan's lie now gave that tree attractiveness. She believed his words, spoken through a lowly snake, above those of her Creator. We read:

³⁰ "Consequently the woman saw that the tree was good for food and that it was something to be longed for to the eyes, yes, the tree was desirable to look upon. So she began taking of its fruit and eating it."—Genesis 3:6.

EVE DECEIVED

³¹ Why was Eve not dumbfounded, and why did she not flee when the serpent, surprisingly, *spoke* to her? The Bible does not say. It is possible that

29, 30. In what way did Eve regard the fruit of the 'tree of knowledge' before Satan lied, and how did she view it after the lie?
31. What may have been Eve's reasoning as the serpent spoke to her?

she saw the serpent at the tree, and its actions may have attracted her attention. She knew that it was a most cautious animal. So the serpent may have appeared very wise, and when it spoke it seemed to have special wisdom.

[32] In any case, the lie spoken through this animal convinced her that she would not die upon her eating of the fruit. Instead she believed she would gain special powers—to be like God, free and independent to judge for herself what course to take. She would not be dependent upon or subject to anyone. Certainly she abandoned subjection to her husband, who had stated God's command to her. She went ahead and took the fruit without consulting him.

[33] That is why the apostle Paul stressed submissiveness on the part of the Christian woman. He pointed out that Eve, in thinking she was achieving absolute independence, was actually doing the very opposite and bringing the greatest trouble upon herself. She tried to do that for which she was not fitted. Paul said: "Adam was not deceived, but the woman was *thoroughly deceived* and *came to be in transgression.*" —1 Timothy 2:11-14.

ADAM'S LACK OF FAITH

[34] Since Adam was not deceived, what impelled him to join his wife in the rebellion? He let his desire for his wife, Eve, take priority over his

32, 33. (a) What freedom did Eve think eating the fruit would give her? (b) How was Eve, in running ahead of her husband, actually losing freedom?
34, 35. (a) Adam not being deceived, why did he enter into the rebellion? (b) Why was the problem raised by Eve's sin a greater one for Adam than his everyday problems of taking care of the garden of Eden, and how did he demonstrate weakness of faith?

relationship with God. So when he saw his wife, he took the fruit from her.—Genesis 3:6.

[35] The Bible does not record the words that passed between Adam and Eve. But here a most serious problem was thrown suddenly 'into his lap.' Adam may have had problems to work out in connection with his dominion over animals and cultivating the garden, but this situation with Eve was something that reached right into his heart and tested his loyalty. He may have wondered: 'Why does such a thing have to happen so suddenly and shockingly to me, in the midst of a happy life? Why did God let this occur?' His faith in God was tested. He should have shown superior love for God. He should have known that God would stand by him.—Psalm 34:15.

[36] Certainly God would have taken care of his son Adam had Adam proved loyal. He would have worked out matters to Adam's complete happiness. (Compare Psalm 22:4, 5.) But Adam did not exercise this faith. Furthermore, he tried to excuse himself, saying: "The woman whom you gave to be with me, she gave me fruit from the tree and so I ate."—Genesis 3:12.

[37] Adam's self-excusing reply blamed the woman as the guilty one. But Adam was fully responsible, and, as head of his household, he was the one with whom God dealt directly. He was reprehensible. Actually, Adam took the course described at James 1:13-15:

[38] "When under trial, let no one say: 'I am being tried by God.' For with evil things God cannot be

36, 37. (a) How, in addition to lack of faith, did Adam reveal that he was self-excusing? (b) But was he fully responsible for his rebellion?
38. How does James 1:13-15 describe the process by which the perfect humans Adam and Eve came to sin?

tried nor does he himself try anyone. But each one is tried by being drawn out and enticed by his own desire. Then the desire, when it has become fertile, gives birth to sin; in turn, sin, when it has been accomplished, brings forth death."

ENTIRE HUMAN RACE HURT

[39] Adam thereby became a sinner. According to the meaning of the Hebrew word for "sin" he 'missed the mark.' He could no longer measure up to perfect standards. He died spiritually and also began to die physically in that day. Adam now had a lack, a moral weakness that also affected him physically, for "the sting producing death is sin." (1 Corinthians 15:56) Adam's spirituality being ruined, his mental workings were unbalanced, and this contributed toward unbalance and deterioration of his physical body. Adam had to die. (Genesis 3:19) He could not pass on full strength morally or physically to his children, for he no longer had it to give. Consequently, "all have sinned and fall short of the glory of God," which Adam had once reflected in his perfection. —Romans 3:23.

[40] Being a sinner, Adam had no right to enjoy communion with Jehovah God. He had no right to live any longer in the paradise garden. God then evidently spoke to his firstborn heavenly Son. This Son had been used by Jehovah in the creative work. (Colossians 1:13, 15, 17) Jehovah said: " 'Here the man has become like one of us

39. (a) In what way did Adam die "in the day" he sinned? (Genesis 2:17) (b) How did his loss of spirituality affect him physically, and also affect his children?
40. (a) Why did Jehovah God put Adam out of the garden of Eden after Adam sinned? (b) What similar action is taken by Christian congregations today, as shown at 1 Corinthians 5:11-13?

in knowing good and bad, and now in order that he may not put his hand out and actually take fruit also from the tree of life and eat and live to time indefinite,—' With that Jehovah God put him out of the garden of Eden to cultivate the ground from which he had been taken." (Genesis 3:22, 23) Similarly today, the Scriptures command that a bad or immoral person who is unrepentant must be disfellowshiped from communion and association with the Christian congregation.—1 Corinthians 5:11-13.

⁴¹ What did all of this mean for the human race? The result was inherited weakness. And yet no person can rightly blame all the bad things he does on this fact, for, actually, all may sin willfully and so bear individual responsibility. In the human race sin has multiplied, so that its extreme badness—with all the pains and sorrow it brings—has been manifest. Sin has ruled like a king over humankind, permeating nearly all thoughts and actions; there is an ingrained selfishness.—Romans 5:14.

GOD'S REACTION TO THE CHALLENGE

⁴² Happily, because of God's undeserved kindness and his love for the human race, he did not abandon mankind so that they would go permanently into extinction. Think, however, of the position in which God was placed: His rulership, his sovereignty, was challenged as to its *rightfulness,* its *righteousness* and *deservedness.* According to the Devil, Jehovah was not ruling through love. He claimed that the reason why God's intel-

41. Since everyone inherited weakness, can anyone blame all his bad acts on this fact? (Romans 3:23; 5:12)
42. (a) What was challenged with regard to God's rulership or sovereignty? (b) What was the Devil's contention or argument about this?

ligent creatures were obedient was not that they loved God's rulership and preferred it above all others. No, he held that God's sovereignty derived its support from others only as the result of His giving every good thing to those obeying Him— that He ruled, in effect, by a form of bribery. (Job 1:9-11) Moreover, the Devil charged that God was keeping something from His creatures that they had a right to have. One of these withheld things was complete, separate independence from Him, the right to act just as they please. —Genesis 3:5.

43 God knew that his rulership was right. He could have destroyed the Devil then and there. But this would not have settled the issue that had been raised. For Satan's challenge, supported by Adam and Eve, not only slandered God's name and government; it also put a shadow on the name of every intelligent person in the universe. So, for the sake of his own name as king, and for the sake of all his family of faithful persons living then and in the future, God permitted wickedness to continue for a limited time.

44 If God had put Adam and Eve to death immediately, none of us who have lived on earth would ever have been born. Even though Adam and Eve had turned bad, God knew that not all their descendants would do so. Many would serve God through all the tests that the Devil could bring. God therefore allowed Satan, as an outlaw, to continue, and he permitted Adam and Eve to bring forth children. Many of their descendants

---

43. Why did the Almighty God not destroy the Devil then and there, but permit wickedness to continue for a time?
44. (a) Where would we who are living be today if God had put Adam and Eve to death immediately? (b) What confidence did God have in men who would come to be born, and has this confidence proved to be justified?

have proved faithful, as the Bible record testifies. —Hebrews, chapter 11.

[45] Even though conditions have been adverse, humanity has, for the most part, been happy to enjoy a measure of life. Actually, few persons have suffered for more than a comparatively few years of their lives. So in spite of hardships, most people are glad that they have been born. However, Je-

---

45. (a) In God's allowance of wickedness, who has suffered for the longest time? (b) Who really has benefited from God's permission of wickedness for a time?

When a court case has been fairly tried, the ruling sets a precedent. In like manner, when the supreme court of heaven decides the universal issue, all creation will benefit

hovah God has tolerated these bad things, observing wickedness and suffering, for about 6,000 years. As a Father to his universal family, this has grieved him. (Compare Psalm 78:40.) He had the power to stop wickedness at any time, but held back for a purpose, not for his personal benefit, but for that of intelligent creatures of the universe now and for all time to come. (Luke 18:7, 8; Job 35:6-8) World history and the Bible indicate that the issue is near to its time of complete settlement.

⁴⁶ There was a legal reason for God's action. For example, when a case has been carried to the Supreme Court of the land and there argued out and fully decided, the Supreme Court's ruling stands as a precedent for deciding that same question in all individual cases thereafter. So, too, this universal issue, settled in the Supreme Court of heaven, will serve as a precedent. Never again will wickedness, with its attendant suffering, be allowed to disturb the universe. We are given a view of Jehovah's Court at Daniel 7:9, 10.

⁴⁷ God has therefore permitted wickedness and suffering for the settlement of the issue of his universal sovereignty. And in settling the issue, God has also made provision for lifting the human race out of its sad condition. This provision will erase all the harm done by the rule of sin as king over the human race. How God has made this provision is the interesting subject for our consideration in Chapter 6.

---

46. What benefit will be gained by letting the issue of God's rulership be fully tested out, even though it has taken about 6,000 years?
47. Along with settling the universal issue of the rightness of his sovereignty, what else has God provided?

God Comes
to Mankind's Rescue

JEHOVAH GOD, in harmony with the dignity of his universal rulership, works out seemingly impossible problems in a marvelous way. And after seeing the outcome, we say, 'It just couldn't have been done in any other way and have been so thorough, righteous and altogether good.' (See Isaiah 55:9.) So, as the Bible shows, at the very time that the challenge to the rightness of his rule was made, God revealed that he would come to the rescue of the human race when he announced: "He [the seed] will bruise you [Satan] in the head." (Genesis 3:15) As time went on, God would let men see the outworking of his purpose.

² Who particularly would be designated by God to be the "seed," eventually to crush Satan's head? Jehovah's only-begotten Son! He was chosen as the one to serve for the primary settlement of the issue regarding the worthiness and righteousness of Jehovah's rulership or sovereignty. Why this great one who was so close to Jehovah's heart? Well, when Satan made his challenge it called into question the loyalty of all persons in the universe, right up to this Son of God. More than that, the question of loyalty would focus more on him than on any other one of God's crea-

1. What confidence can we have that God will come to the rescue of the human race?
2, 3. (a) Who was designated by Jehovah God to be the promised "seed"? (b) For what reasons was he the logical one to be chosen?

tures, because he was the chief Son of Jehovah, next to Him in the universe. He had been co-worker with God in making the universe. (Colossians 1:15-17) A challenger of God could say, 'Of all the creatures who would be faithful in serving God, he should be.' So Satan's challenge brought this mighty Son of God into the limelight.

3 Furthermore, in the Proverbs, chapter eight, this Son, personified as wisdom, says, speaking of God's creative work: "The things I was fond of were with the sons of men." (Vs. 31) He deeply *loved* mankind. He gladly took this assignment to vindicate his Father, first out of loyalty to Him and, additionally, out of the love that he had for mankind.

4 Now, in Jehovah God's love for humankind, could he condone the wickedness that Satan, along with Adam, had brought into the universe? Could God say to any sinning individual, 'Well, I like you and want to show you mercy, so I'll just overlook your sin'? In harmony with his justice and righteousness he could not ignore sin and let it go unaccounted for. If he should do this, he would be undermining the foundation of his government.—Psalm 89:14.

5 We have an example of the results of being "soft" with, and, in effect, condoning lawlessness, in some nations of earth today. They have in many cases been slack and not zealous to act against wrongdoers. Criminals have been let run loose. The result has been that people lose faith in the governments and everything finally breaks down. The Universal Ruler will not let that take place with his laws.

---

4. Why could God not ignore sin or let it go unaccounted for?
5. What happens to government when lawlessness is condoned or lawbreakers are allowed to get by with their lawbreaking?

⁶ Accordingly, Jehovah the Universal Sovereign, in his responsibility to uphold law and order in the universe, does not overlook sin. "God is not one to be mocked." (Galatians 6:7) At Habakkuk 1:13, the prophet says to Jehovah: "You are too pure in eyes to see what is bad; and to look on trouble you are not able. Why is it that you look on those dealing treacherously?" Only for a good purpose and for a relatively short time has he let wrongdoing take place. Really, the way that God has decided on is the *only* way that he can genuinely help mankind.

A LEGAL PROBLEM

⁷ Adam had sold his future offspring, without their consent, into slavery to sin and death. The price he received for the "sale" was the selfish doing of what he wanted to do, stepping out in rebellion against God. (Romans 7:14) Man's helplessness in getting free from enslavement to death is expressed in the forty-ninth Psalm, verses six to nine: "Those who are trusting in their means of maintenance, and who keep boasting about the abundance of their riches, not one of them can by any means redeem even a brother, nor give to God a ransom for him; (and the redemption price of their soul is so precious that it has ceased to time indefinite) that he should still live forever and not see the pit." The price was too precious, too high, beyond the reach of all mankind. As far as imperfect man's ability was concerned, relief was so far away that it was "to time indefinite," actually beyond hope. So,

6. How do the prophet Habakkuk and the apostle Paul point out that God does not overlook sin?
7. (a) How did Adam "sell" humankind into slavery to sin and death? (b) How does Psalm 49:6-9 express man's helplessness to deliver himself?

if man was ever to be delivered, God had to act to make provision.—Compare Psalm 79:9.

[8] In order to have dealings with those who were born in sin, though it was through no fault of their own, God had to have some legal basis on which to deal with them. (Psalm 51:5; Romans 5:12) Otherwise, all men would have to die forever, since God's law required that sinners be removed from the universe. Only the sacrifice of another man, a perfect one, as a "precious" price, could buy back what Adam had lost.—1 Timothy 2:5, 6.

[9] Accordingly, Jehovah needed someone—one whose sacrifice would be the legal basis—through whom he could deal. Just as a human government could not properly negotiate with criminals, so Jehovah God could not deal directly with sinful people and still maintain the dignity and righteousness of his government.

[10] By establishing this legal basis, Jehovah would be able to demonstrate the rightness of his universal rulership, showing also the extreme badness of sin. At the same time he could show mercy to humans. The apostle Paul expresses it:

[11] "For all have sinned and fall short of the glory of God, and it is as a free gift that they are being declared righteous by his undeserved kindness through the release by the ransom paid by Christ Jesus. God set him forth as an offering for propitiation through faith in his blood. This was in order to exhibit his own righteousness, because he was forgiving the sins that occurred in the past while God was exercising forbearance; so as to

8, 9. In order to maintain the dignity and righteousness of his government, what did Jehovah God have to do to help humankind?

10, 11. In forgiving sins and declaring people righteous, how did God demonstrate (a) his own righteousness and justice? (b) the badness of sin, and his own mercy?

exhibit his own righteousness in this present season, that he might be righteous even when declaring righteous the man that has faith in Jesus."—Romans 3:23-26.

¹² We could illustrate, from everyday life, the reasonableness and legality of God's dealings. Say that a man, a householder, has an upright, clean, obedient family. He knows of a young man in jail, with a large fine against him, for some wrong that he has done. This young man has been in bad company and has learned bad ways. However, the man believes that he can help the prisoner and eventually rehabilitate him. In justice to

12. What problems confront a man who desires mercifully to bring an "undesirable" into his family as a member? (Romans 5:8)

Before welcoming a wayward young stranger as a member of his household, the man of the house would want him to get cleaned up

himself and his clean, respectable family, he cannot bring him immediately into his home and make his family associate with the young man in this condition. What, then, can he do to help?

[13] The man could get a friend to pay the fine that would release the court's judgment against the prisoner and get the court to give him custody. After proper training and discipline of the young man the friend could turn him over to the householder in a condition of rehabilitation, so that he could be accepted as a clean, respectable member of the household. Thus all legal requirements would be fully met. The householder would have been completely just and righteous in his dealings, and mercy would have been shown to the young man.

[14] Actually, God deals with the human family through his Son, Jesus Christ, who acts as Jehovah's representative in the matter. Those obedient to God's arrangement come to have a legal standing with Him. They are redeemed and reconciled or brought into harmony with God. (Colossians 1:13, 14, 20) They gain a personal relationship and are able to call upon Him as "Father."—Matthew 6:9.

GOD'S SON COMES TO EARTH

[15] God's Son, therefore, was sent to earth—to become a human, born of a woman. He could serve for the test of integrity here on earth, where the issue was raised. He could also be the ransom price for humankind. By miraculous birth through

---

13. What steps could the man take to make the young man a fitting and legal member of his household?
14. On what basis does God reconcile the human family to himself?
15. Why did God's Son have to be sent to earth?

the virgin Mary he became a human son of God.
—Galatians 4:4.

[16] This son was born of an imperfect woman,
but was himself perfect and unblemished. His
perfect life was transferred from the heavenly,
spirit realm to Mary's womb. The angel Gabriel
had announced to Mary: "Holy spirit will come
upon you, and power of the Most High will over-
shadow you. For that reason also what is born
will be called holy, God's Son." (Luke 1:35) The
holy spirit of God put a wall of invisible power
around Mary, so that Jesus Christ would be born
a perfect baby. Satan the Devil would, of course,
have desired to destroy or damage that Son before he was born, if possible. Consider his later
attempts to kill Jesus, as revealed at Matthew
2:7-16 and Luke 4:28-30.

[17] Jesus, throughout his entire human life, remained in that perfect state. He was "loyal, guile-
less, undefiled, separated from the sinners." (Hebrews 7:26) Jesus' life course on earth settled
the question of integrity to God beyond doubt,
perfectly, completely. He said, before his sacrificial
death: "The ruler of the world is coming. And he
has no hold on me," and, "Now there is a judging
of this world; now the ruler of this world [the
Devil] will be cast out." (John 14:30; 12:31;
2 Corinthians 4:4) Satan was never able to make
Jesus Christ give in under pressure, therefore he
had no hold on Jesus, no valid charge that he
could bring against Jesus. Jesus had "conquered
the world" by refusing to fall into sin with it.
—John 16:33; 8:46.

---

16. (a) How was Jesus born as a perfect child when he had an
imperfect mother? (b) Why did Jesus, when a child, and also
later, need special protection?
17. How do the Scriptures show that Jesus maintained his
perfection right down to his death?

[18] The apostle Paul declared of Jesus: "He learned obedience from the things he suffered; and after he had been made perfect he became responsible for everlasting salvation to all those obeying him." (Hebrews 5:8, 9) So it was on Christ's *own merit* that God declared him righteous at the end of his earthly course. He was resurrected to life in the spirit, "declared righteous in spirit." (1 Timothy 3:16) He was qualified and installed in heaven as the perfect High Priest on mankind's behalf. God did not have to grant righteousness to Christ as a *gift,* for as a sinless human, he both had and retained a righteous standing with God from start to finish. That was why Jesus' sacrifice was perfect and could serve as a basis for other men to be declared righteous. If others are declared righteous it is not on grounds of their own righteousness, but it is on the basis of the atonement sacrifice of Jesus Christ. In their case it is indeed a gift to them.—Romans 5:17.

[19] By this faithful course Jesus qualified to become the advocate of all who desire to serve God. The apostle John wrote: "If anyone does commit a sin, we have a helper [or, advocate] with the Father, Jesus Christ, a righteous one. And he is a propitiatory [covering] sacrifice for our sins." (1 John 2:1, 2) He is also called a "mediator between God and men." (1 Timothy 2:5) The Devil has tried to find fault with God's servants from the time of Abel the son of Adam. Satan is called "the accuser of our brothers . . .

18. (a) Why was Jesus' righteousness when he was on earth not a gift? (b) If anyone else of humankind is declared righteous, why is it a free gift?
19. What position does Jesus hold with respect to those who want to serve God?

who accuses them day and night before our God."
—Revelation 12:10.

[20] So, in the legal contest, Jesus Christ has
appeared before God as an advocate at law. When
faithful servants of God have made a mistake,
committed a sin, Jesus has presented evidence
before God as the Judge that they are not worthy
of death—that his propitiatory sacrifice covers
their mistakes and sins. He has shown that their
intent was to do right even in the face of their
imperfection. (Romans 7:15-19) He has called
attention to their acts of faith and their calling
on God in true repentance when they have sinned.
(Hebrews 6:10) They do this all on the basis
of Jesus' sacrifice. (John 16:23) And God accepts
Jesus' intercession for them.

HOW JESUS GETS "CHILDREN"

[21] When Jesus was on earth as a man he had
the power to have a family of his own by natural
human means. He did not bring forth that family,
but gave up that potential in his sacrifice. As he
said: "The Son of man came, not to be ministered
to, but to minister and to give his soul a ransom
in exchange for many." (Matthew 20:28) Jesus
therefore became the "last Adam." Adam brought
forth a family, an imperfect one, with bad traits.
Jesus Christ brings forth a family that attains to
righteousness. Individuals can transfer from the
family of Adam and be regenerated through the
righteousness of Jesus Christ, and, by putting on
the new personality, can come to be 'in his image.'

---

20. As advocate and mediator, what has Jesus done in behalf
of God's servants?
21. (a) How did Jesus, the one man, give his soul "a ransom in
exchange for many"? (b) Why is he known as the "last Adam"?

They can be cleaned up as sons of the "last Adam." —1 Corinthians 15:45, 49.

²² Isaiah the prophet, by inspiration, described some of Christ's sufferings and said, speaking to Jehovah: "If you will set his soul as a guilt offering, he will see his offspring." (Isaiah 53:10) Christ does not get offspring through the natural method. But as the "Eternal Father" he brings forth a family with his traits, in the manner that Isaiah describes, because Jehovah

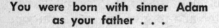

You were born with sinner Adam as your father . . .

"set his soul as a guilt offering" for humankind. (Isaiah 9:6) We must keep in mind, however, that Jesus Christ, after bringing them to human perfection, turns purchased and rehabilitated humankind over to Jehovah God, "the Father, to whom every family in heaven and on earth owes its name."—Ephesians 3:14, 15; 1 Corinthians 15:26, 28.

22. (a) How does Isaiah 53:10 show the means by which Christ comes to have children? (b) Does Christ forever keep these children for his very own, or what?

RANSOM COUNTERACTS SIN

23 Summing up the matter, we can say that the ransom provided through God's Son counteracts the sin of Adam. Adam's sin brought everybody down. The ransom, of course, does not save every last human soul, but counteracts the effects of the sin innate in us. How? Every last soul who wants to get free from sin and imperfection *can* get these wiped out and become wholly clean. Even those resurrected from the dead will have the opportunity to avail them-

23. How can it be said that the ransom provided through Jesus Christ counteracts sin?

. . . But you can choose Jesus as your "Eternal Father"

selves of the ransom. (Acts 24:15) Those who do not get life will be persons who do not want Jehovah's rule over them. They do not love righteousness and hate lawlessness. They are self-condemned, adding their own willful sin to their inherited sin.—John 3:17-21, 36.

[24] Therefore Christ's atonement sacrifice, administered by his Kingdom rule, completely wipes out what Adam did. The last enemy, death (the death brought to mankind by the sin of Adam), will be brought to nothing. When death is wiped out, then all that Adam did—all that he brought on the human race—will not be here at all. There will not be anything at all left to show for Adam's sin. (1 Corinthians 15:26, 55-57) And there will be nothing left to show for the sin of the Devil, because, as the Bible says: "For this purpose the Son of God was made manifest, namely, to break up the works of the Devil." (1 John 3:8) Satan will have completely wasted his effort and lost his life. The shadow on the name of God will be totally erased. God's name will be fully vindicated to all eternity and those who want his sovereignty will be there, alive, to his praise.—Psalm 150.

[25] What loving-kindness of God! And what love on the part of the Lord Jesus Christ! We can say with the apostle: "O the depth of God's riches and wisdom and knowledge! How unsearchable his judgments are and past tracing out his ways

----

24. (a) In the end, will there be anything to show as an "accomplishment" of the rebellious act of Adam? (b) Will Satan's efforts leave any lasting mark on the universe?
25. How should our hearts respond as we see what God has done to rescue humankind?

are!" (Romans 11:33) Regardless of what things the world may bring to cause doubts and assail our faith, through our having a true appreciation of these things we can exclaim, 'Such a God is fully deserving of our complete devotion and service!'—See Philippians 3:8, 9.

Chapter 7

The Source
and Sustainer of Life

HAVING arranged the way for men and women to get free from sin and imperfection, can Jehovah God thereafter keep them alive? Is there real assurance that a person who makes Jehovah his God can live an endless life in health and happiness?

² Because of God's ability to create he would certainly have the ability to sustain the earth itself. If necessary, he could constantly renew the power of the sun. As for the earth, he has made it a self-sustaining "spaceship," "recycling" its wastes and ever renewing its face. Forests and streams, if left to themselves, in a short time refresh themselves and erase any damage caused by ruinous works of man.

---

1. What questions arise when considering whether to make Jehovah one's God?
2. Does God, who created the universe, also have the ability to keep it operating forever?

³ What about humans on earth? King Solomon, a great observer of life, said: "A generation is going, and a generation is coming; but the earth is standing even to time indefinite." (Ecclesiastes 1:4; 1 Corinthians 7:31) Solomon was not saying that it would always be this way with human generations. He was talking about the vanity of life as it is in the present system of things, with "king" death ruling. If you read the book of Ecclesiastes, you will note that Solomon was giving wise counsel as to living *during this time.* He was basically saying that we should not put our hope in the present world system, its material things and its ways.

⁴ After describing mankind's present condition, Solomon reports the results of his investigation, saying: "The conclusion of the matter, everything having been heard, is: Fear the true God and keep his commandments. For this is the whole obligation of man." (Ecclesiastes 12:13) And Jesus, the one greater than Solomon, explained: "This means everlasting life, their taking in knowledge of you, the only true God, and of the one whom you sent forth, Jesus Christ."—John 17:3.

⁵ Will it not be a fine thing when you can associate with loved friends and relatives, knowing you will not have to endure the sadness of losing them? Can this be possible?

⁶ It is not only possible—it is altogether sure, because "Jehovah is in truth God. He is the *living*

3, 4. (a) Do King Solomon's words at Ecclesiastes 1:4 contradict the idea that humans can live forever? Explain. (b) How does Solomon's conclusion, together with the words of Jesus, show that our life, even in this calamitous world, need not be a vain or hopeless one?
5, 6. (a) Why is it possible for a person to live forever? (b) What is it about the human makeup that proves there is a living Creator with a good purpose toward us?

God and the King to time indefinite." (Jeremiah 10:10) Moses, in prayer, spoke of God's eternal existence, saying: "Even from time indefinite to time indefinite you are God." (Psalm 90:2) God, living forever, can begin life and keep it going forever. The fact that mankind exists with the qualities of imagination, appreciation of beauty, kindness, love and other emotions, proves that man has a living Creator and that He has a good purpose toward humankind. In a world operated by chance, or by blind forces, emotion would have no place. No, life must have a *living source*.

"SPONTANEOUS LIFE" A FALLACY

7 In 1864 Louis Pasteur, the renowned scientist to whom medicine and surgery owe much, said in a lecture at the Sorbonne, a famous Paris college:

8 "Gentlemen, I would point to that [sterile] liquid and say to you, I have taken my drop of water from the immensity of creation, and I have taken it full of the elements fitted for the development of inferior beings. And I wait, I watch, I question it, begging it to recommence for me the beautiful spectacle of the first creation. But it is dumb —dumb ever since these experiments were begun several years ago; it is dumb because I have kept it from the only thing which man cannot produce —from the germs which feed in the air—from life, for life is a germ and a germ is life. Never will the doctrine of spontaneous generation recover from the mortal blow of this simple experiment."

9 That statement was made more than a hundred years ago, and it is true today. Never have scientists been able to cause life to arise spontaneously out of material that was not already

7, 8. How did Louis Pasteur prove that life cannot come of itself from inanimate material?
9. How do scientists and other practical persons today show their faith in Pasteur's discovery?

living. In fact, doctors, dentists, surgeons and scientists rely on—have faith in—Pasteur's experiment. They sterilize their hospital and surgical instruments; they pasteurize milk and sterilize water, so that germs may not be there to cause infection or spoilage. Of what use would such processes be if life could originate in a sterile medium? How long would the world keep on spending millions of dollars on the process if it were found to be ineffective and unreliable?

¹⁰ Consequently, all evidence points to a source of life that is itself *alive*. The Bible says of Jehovah God: "With you is the source of life." (Psalm 36:9) Someone may ask, 'If life must exist to beget life, who created God?' But this is merely pushing the answer farther away—a form of evasion in facing up to the question. Inconsistently, such persons seem to have no trouble believing that inanimate matter always existed.

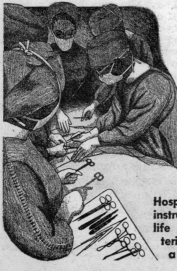

10. (a) How does the Bible point us to the source of life? (b) What is a person doing who asks, 'Who created God?'

Hospitals sterilize surgical instruments. Why? Because life (infection-causing bacteria) cannot originate in a sterile medium

AN INFINITE CREATOR

[11] Surely we could not expect that the Creator of the vast universe would be thoroughly understood by his creatures. (Romans 11:34) Nevertheless, there is at least the conception of "infinity" in science and mathematics. We can imagine infinite space, and as far as astronomers can tell, the universe may be infinite, boundless. The farther their telescopes enable them to see, the more galaxies they behold.

[12] Then, going in the other direction, into the infinitesimally small, physicists still cannot find the ultimate particle. When the atom was discovered, it appeared simple: The atom was the indivisible particle, scientists thought. Experiments with the atom, however, have shown their theory to be a fallacy. The list of particles, or supposed particles, making up the atom has grown quite long, and the end is not yet.

[13] Can we not, then, conceive of a God who had no beginning—who existed forever? This is what he declares of himself. (Deuteronomy 32:40; Romans 16:26) If we accept this claim from God, we can believe that he could infuse life into persons who obey him, and could sustain that life forever.

EARTH'S CYCLES FOR MAN'S BENEFIT

[14] Some persons ask: 'What about the fact that all living things tend to deteriorate?—that the cells and tissues break down, so that old age sets

---

11, 12. What things demonstrate the truth that we cannot expect to understand everything about our majestic Creator? (Isaiah 40:18, 22)
13. If we accept God's words at Deuteronomy 32:40, what can we believe about our own existence?
14. When we see deterioration and death all around us, what question naturally arises as to our own life?

OXYGEN CYCLE

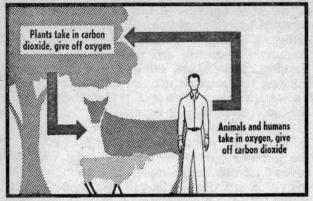

Plants take in carbon dioxide, give off oxygen

Animals and humans take in oxygen, give off carbon dioxide

in, culminating in death? Would not this always continue to take place with human life?' Let us see.

15 All physical things on earth tend to break down with age. Rocks crumble. Wood decays. Think, though, what the situation would be if there were no effect of weather on rocks, wood, and other material, and if there were no decay of organic matter. That would mean that the earth would be sterile. Few, if any, chemical reactions could take place. Our digestive systems could not function properly, because they operate by chemical and bacterial action, breaking down and changing the composition of food. Little work could be done, because few things could be altered in structure. Even now certain plastics that are not easily decomposed are causing a waste-disposal problem.

15. What would be the situation on earth if nothing decayed, broke down, or changed in its composition?

¹⁶ For earthly life to continue, then, there must be changes in organic and inorganic matter. Cycles of birth and death were originally purposed for every living thing on earth, with the exception of mankind. Why except mankind? Because man was made in God's image and likeness. Only humans, not animals, can be called God's "sons" and "daughters." Not of animals, but of man, it is said that 'death entered in through sin.'—Genesis 1:27; Romans 5:12.

¹⁷ Consider some of these cycles. There is plant

---

16. (a) What changes in matter are essential for life to exist on earth? (b) In what way is man different from animals with regard to the reason that humans die?
17, 18. What are some of the cycles essential to the continuance of life on earth?

NITROGEN CYCLE

Lightning combines nitrogen with oxygen. Rain brings this to earth

Green plants provide food for animals and humans

Bacteria act on decaying plants and animal manure, release nitrogen back into air. Other bacteria produce plant food

Bacteria take nitrogen from the air for plants' use

life that provides food for all animal life, and, in fact, is the basis for all earthly life. Plants can do something that animals cannot—they manufacture their own food by the use of sunlight. This process is called "photosynthesis." Animal life must therefore depend on plant life. Plants must grow, supply food and die. Then, through the marvel of seed germination, another crop is produced.

[18] In the sea the "food chain" maintains life on various levels; the tiny vegetable phytoplankton are food for the animal zooplankton, which, in turn, feed the larger fish, including some that serve as food for man. Then bacterial action converts dead matter into food for the phytoplankton, and the cycle begins all over again.

[19] In the process, individual animals die, to be replaced by offspring, thus preserving the species. What, then, is the hope for continued individual human existence? Is there a difference in this respect between man and animals?

[20] Yes, there is. For, while cells and tissues in living bodies suffer wear, and some cells die, life tends to reverse the "running-down" process. Living things make highly organized, complex compounds out of more simple ones. If the life-force could be kept operating at full efficiency, worn tissues would continually be replaced or repaired. Old age would not set in, and the person would never die. Only the Creator can accomplish this in humans. He promises everlasting life to obedient men and women. All the earth's cycles— among them the birth and death of plant and animal life—are actually arranged primarily for mankind's ultimate benefit.

19, 20. Explain how, even though cells and tissues break down, a human could live forever.

[21] The Bible record reveals that humans were made to live much longer than animals. The early offspring of Adam, being near to perfection, lived as long as 969 years. This illustrates the fact that cell-replacement continued for all those years, and the cells of the central nervous system (which scientists say can be repaired but not replaced) were maintained in healthy repair during centuries of living. (Genesis 5:27; see also verses 5-31; 9:29.) The short-lived generations of today are, of course, far removed from that time, with sin and imperfection multiplying during the thousands of years since. The human race has deteriorated, but God can infuse power into those who look to him, so that they may live to time indefinite.—Isaiah 40:29-31.

"THE BREAD OF LIFE"

[22] Now, long before man appeared on the earth, animals were dying, as is attested to by fossil discoveries. They were created with a limited life-span. But humankind was created, though from the same elements, of a much finer nature, a higher order.

[23] Of humans, not of animals, it is said that God put 'time indefinite into their heart.' (Ecclesiastes 3:11) Only humans have a sense of the past and of the future. Only humans possess a capacity for spirituality, that is, to take in knowledge of God, to partake of his spiritual qualities and moral excellence. (Hebrews 12:9) Since God

21. (a) What evidence do we have that, even with imperfection, human life was once much longer than it is in our time? (b) Why is man's life-span shorter now than in the earliest periods of mankind's history?
22, 23. (a) Why do animals die? (b) How has God constructed humans with a far superior organism? (c) Of all earth's creatures, what unique quality do humans possess? (d) What is required on man's part to keep living to time indefinite?

provided this spiritual capacity for humankind, it must be filled, satisfied, for the human to function properly—to keep on living. Jesus said: "Happy are those conscious of their spiritual need."—Matthew 5:3.

24 Jesus Christ, even though he was a perfect man on earth, depended on God for sustained life. He said: "*My food* is for me to do the will of him that sent me and to finish his [God's] work." He further said: "I live because of the Father." (John 4:34; 6:57) He spoke of himself, saying: "I am the bread of life. Your forefathers ate the manna in the wilderness and yet died. . . . If anyone eats of this bread he will live forever." —John 6:48-51.

25 Of course, Jesus Christ did not mean that men would eat his literal body of flesh. But by exercising faith in the atoning sacrifice of Christ and by "eating" the spiritual food that God provides by means of Christ, one can live forever. When? In the "new earth," under Christ's Kingdom rule. Then he as High Priest, along with his associate kings and underpriests,* will apply his atoning sacrifice fully to obedient ones on earth. As a result, their bodies will be healed. Then, continuing to do God's will, they will live forever.—John 3:16.

26 Jehovah sent his only-begotten Son to earth

---

* See Chapters 12 and 15. Also see *The Truth That Leads to Eternal Life,* published by Watchtower Bible and Tract Society of New York, Inc., 117 Adams St., Brooklyn, New York 11201.

24. How did Jesus, a perfect man, explain what kept his life sustained?
25. What did Jesus mean by his words at John 6:48-51?
26. (a) Is it reasonable to suppose that God would let his Son suffer and die so that people might live better only *temporarily?* (b) What offer, on what terms, does Jehovah hold out to all persons?

at the greatest cost to himself. He would never let his Son suffer and die to provide a better life for merely a *short period of time*. He says to all: "Turn away from what is bad and do what is good, and so reside to time indefinite. For Jehovah is a lover of justice, and he will not leave his loyal ones. To time indefinite they will certainly be guarded." (Psalm 37:27, 28) Yes, Jehovah is the sustaining Source of life and the grand Guardian of life forever for all who continue in obedience to him.

Chapter 8

Outstanding Gifts That Reveal the God of Love

HOW do we know that God is good? Why could not the Almighty God just as well be bad, or at least have some bad in him? How do we know he has an altogether benevolent attitude and purpose toward humankind?

[2] These are questions that might run through a person's mind when he considers the psalmist's statement: "Good and upright is Jehovah," and Jesus' words: "Nobody is good, except one, God." —Psalm 25:8; Mark 10:18.

[3] For God to be good, he certainly must be a God who cares about his creation, every part of

1, 2. What questions might a person think of when he reads the Bible statements at Psalm 25:8 and Mark 10:18?
3-5. (a) What quality would be required for God to be good? (b) What two things would he have to provide for his intelligent creatures? Why?

it. First, he would be a God who makes arrangements for its subsistence.

[4] Second, if God is good he must supply more than the mere physical things his creation needs just to keep living. This would be particularly so in the case of humanity, for humans want more out of life than mere existence. God's intelligent creatures obviously are not made to carry on a drab, monotonous life. So God must provide arrangements for feeding the mind through the five senses. People use these senses for more than keeping alive. They possess the ability to appreciate and enjoy their surroundings. People, in fact, feel pity for a person who is deprived of his sight, hearing or senses of smell and taste, because he is missing pleasures that add to the zest of living.

[5] Man's home the earth should, accordingly, have the things that make life joyous. Is this what the facts show?

THINGS THAT DELIGHT US

[6] Consider the miracle of a fruit tree. Such trees are literally fruit "factories." Their boughs are burdened with an amazing crop of their nutritious products. And these fruit "factories" operate quietly and without pollution, smoke, radiation or disturbance. As they produce food, they are at the same time a delight to the eye. It is a pleasure to stroll through an orchard. The trees provide *cooling shade,* as well as *refreshment for the atmosphere,* giving off *oxygen* and, often, *exhilarating fragrance.*

[7] In addition, their fruit is *more than mere sustenance.* It is delicious, a joy to eat, as is all

6, 7. How are fruit trees an evidence of the goodness of God?

food that God has provided. What human could ever conceive of or invent the flavor of a peach, an orange, a cherry, an apple, a banana or a mango? At best man can make only poor imitations.

8 Music is another wonderful gift. It can calm the spirit. It can lift one to the heights of ecstasy. It can cause one to meditate soberly or seriously. It can spur one to action. Certain musical strains recall memories of pleasant places and events.

9 Who can explain exactly why music should

8, 9. How can music be none other than a special gift from a benevolent God?

God gave us beautiful sunsets, the smell of flowers, the flavor of food, enjoyment of sound —all to add to the pleasure of living have such marked effects on the human mind and heart? That we are able to respond to music, that we have a built-in sense of rhythm and sound distinction so that we can enjoy it, is really an integral gift put into our bodies by a Creator who appreciates beautiful things. Furthermore, those with the talent to produce good music—what pleasure they derive out of this gift of God, being able to entertain their fellowman!

[10] The ability to carry on conversation is one of the most delightful gifts. How terrible it would be if we could not communicate, or if we had only writing, sign language or grunts and growls. The human mind can express itself and find response in conversation more than, for example, in the printed page. Yet, reading and writing are gifts that are also sources of enjoyment.

[11] Then there are gorgeous displays of color throughout creation: The beauteous and endless variety of flowers, the marvelous sunsets that no artist can duplicate, besides innumerable other lovely things on earth in the greatest variety. These hundreds of delights are loving gifts for the most pleasurable use of the senses that we were kindly given.

[12] Still, some who doubt creation may object. They may say, for example, that the fragrance and color of flowers are only for the purpose of filling a necessity, for they attract insects that pollinate the plants. That is no doubt partly true. But if that is the only reason for the existence

10. Would you say that conversation is a gift from a God who made humankind 'in his likeness'? Explain.
11. What are some other gifts that are not essential to mere living, but are so valuable to our enjoyment of life?
12. What can we answer to those who, doubting that there is a Creator, say that the things we enjoy are actually only for functional purposes?

of these outstanding gifts, why is it that they are also a source of human delight? Why do they promote peace of mind and a feeling of well-being in us? And who can name a purely functional reason for beautiful sunsets? Who can say that music is an essential for maintaining existence, and not a pleasure-producing gift?

[13] The fact that many functional things in life are at the same time the source of great comfort and pleasure speaks well of the amazing economy of God, his diverse wisdom and his love for his creatures.

GIFTS THAT WE MAY FAIL TO APPRECIATE

[14] Sometimes we view things that do not appear beautiful to us as unworthy of consideration. This is particularly true of insects, which we may be prone to look upon as "pests." But here again the Creator has done something fine for us. Some of these very things that we despise are actually a provision saving us endless hours of drudgery so that we can have time to enjoy the finer things.

[15] Consider, for example, the earthworm. These little creatures are absolutely harmless. They sometimes number more than two million in one acre of ground. They work incessantly. They move from about seven to as much as eighteen tons (6 to 16 metric tons) of soil per acre (.4 hectare) each year, burrowing to depths of eight feet (2.4 meters) below the surface. Their bodies digest organic matter in the soil, providing a rich source of calcium, magnesium, potassium,

---

13. What can we say about the fact that many of the functional things also are a source of enjoyment?
14. How are we wrongly prone to view things that are not enjoyable to us?
15. What fine work does the lowly earthworm do in our behalf?

phosphorus and nitrates, essential for healthy plant growth. They help to maintain the balance of alkalinity and acidity in the soil. Their burrowing activities bring about aeration and irrigation of the soil and reduce putrefaction. They drag leaves and other vegetation below ground for the enrichment of the soil.

[16] Now, if it were not for the earthworm, it would be up to man to perform all this work. But alas, it would be impossible for the farmer, working day and night, to prepare his land for crops as does the earthworm. And the cost would be far more than the farmer could bear. So just as the fruit trees and vegetation produce for mankind with little or no effort on

16. How do the earthworm and insects free humans for enjoyment of life?

Earthworms perform tasks that no farmer could duplicate

his part, so does the earthworm. In addition, there is the great army of insects, performing many dull, monotonous chores, releasing man for more intellectual, more pleasurable pursuits.

[17] Regarding the services rendered to mankind by insects, Carl D. Duncan, Professor of Entomology and Botany, San Jose State College, said:

[18] "It is not too much to say that insects determine the character of man's world to a far greater extent than he does himself, and that if they were suddenly to disappear completely the world would be changed so extensively that it is extremely doubtful that man would be able to maintain any sort of organized society whatever."

WHAT ABOUT "PESTS"?

[19] Professor Duncan also cited another scientist, Dr. Frank Lutz, as estimating that not more than one half of one percent of all the insects in the United States can be termed "pests."

[20] In considering the problem of "pests," it must be acknowledged that man has brought about an imbalance. His filthiness and pollution have played their part in upsetting the ecology. Sometimes man's killing off certain insects or animals causes an abnormal increase in others. Then, efforts to control such an increase by poisons result in killing the majority, but leaving poison-resistant ones among them to multiply and "take over" the population. This poses a bigger problem, such as the so-called "super rat," which only very strong and dangerous poisons can kill.

17, 18. To what extent do insects work for mankind's good? 19, 20. (a) What has actually been a major factor in bringing about a "pest" problem? (b) What natural process results in added difficulty in killing certain animals, insects and disease bacteria?

Similar problems have been encountered with certain insects and disease bacteria.

[21] When the so-called "pests" are abnormally increased, they leave their proper habitat and overflow into man's personal domain. They invade and destroy man's food supplies and befoul his property. They spread disease, not usually on their own part, but by carrying disease organisms from garbage and sewage. This is especially apparent in big cities, where piles of garbage carelessly thrown about attract and cause multiplication of flies, as well as rats, and now, the "super rats."

[22] But even these lowly creatures perform a service by reason of becoming "pests." Not only do they clean up some of the garbage, but their presence forces man to take some action to keep his surroundings cleaner so that the "pests" will not come around to make his life miserable. In this way there is some curb to man's carelessness, laziness and uncleanness.

[23] The natural "sanitation squad," made up of insects, microorganisms and larger animals, has done other things that man would never have been able to accomplish. These scavengers work to clear the forest floor of the debris of dead branches and trees. They dispose of the carcasses of dead animals. They thus prevent many devastating forest fires and much pollution and disease.

WHY WE CAN BE HAPPY
DESPITE CAUSES FOR GRIEF

[24] All these gifts from God, and many more too

---

21. Why do such "pests" often invade man's domain?
22. How do even "pests" serve to bring a benefit?
23. What good have animals, among them some viewed as "pests," done for humankind?
24. In what ways are the many gifts just discussed evidence that God is happy and wants us to be happy?

numerous to list, lighten man's burden. They also protect him from diseases and give him pleasure. Hence, they are evidences that God is truly good and is for this reason "the happy God." (1 Timothy 1:11) God enjoys life, and his purpose in creation is to share that joy with others. (Revelation 4:11) But can we really be happy in this present system of things, enjoying the life that we have?

[25] In this upset system of things we have sorrows from time to time. But when we understand God's good purposes toward us we can, in the overall sense, be happy.

[26] For example, death may come in a family. It does indeed bring sorrow, for death is an enemy. (1 Corinthians 15:26) But those who believe in God and his goodness will not be overwhelmed by grief. On this point the apostle Paul wrote: "Brothers, we do not want you to be ignorant concerning those who are sleeping in death; that you may not sorrow just as the rest also do who have no hope." Then Paul spoke comfortingly about the resurrection.—1 Thessalonians 4:13.

[27] We may tend, however, to let sorrows completely destroy our happiness. But in this Jehovah God gives us the greatest example. Think about the greatest expression of his goodness when he sent his Son to earth as a man, to die for us. This was something far beyond normal. It was entirely undeserved kindness on Jehovah's part. The apostle calls our attention to the extent of this loving act, saying: "God recommends his own

---

25, 26. Give one example of a sorrow that can be to a great extent overcome by our having a knowledge of God's purposes.
27. What is our greatest example of one continuing happy under distressful circumstances?

love to us in that, while we were yet sinners, Christ died for us." (Romans 5:8) Do you think that this did not cause God grief? What can be more distressful to a father than seeing his own beloved son die? Yet God also gained great happiness in observing his Son's obedience and faithfulness, and his willingness to die for humankind. God was also happy in contemplating the benefits that this sacrifice would bring to us despite the distress it caused to Him and to his Son. (Isaiah 53:10, 12) Indeed, the gift of God's own Son is the greatest expression of love of all!

²⁸ And have you considered the sorrow to Jehovah's heart when he sees humankind, his creation, in distress because they have rejected and disobeyed his laws? When men did bad and brought great distress upon themselves and upon God's servants dwelling among them, God "felt hurt at his heart."—Genesis 6:6.

JESUS, AN EXAMPLE OF HAPPINESS
THROUGH SUFFERING

²⁹ Jesus Christ, when on earth, reflected perfectly his Father's personality and way of doing things. Jesus said: "He that has seen me has seen the Father also." (John 14:9) Therefore, men do not have to see God with their literal eyes to understand him. Did Jesus have times of sorrow? He was prophetically spoken of as "a man meant for pains," and "he was despised, and we held him as of no account." Nonetheless, he was happy in what he was accomplishing. The same prophecy says: "Because of the trouble

---

28. Does mankind's bad condition because of sin have any effect on Jehovah God's feelings?
29. What kind of experience did Jesus have during his life on earth?

of his soul he will see, he will be satisfied . . . [he] will bring a righteous standing to many people."—Isaiah 53:3, 11.

[30] Jesus was often saddened that the people of Israel, who should have known God, were alienated from God by man-made religious traditions. He was "grieved at the insensibility of their hearts." (Mark 3:5) He felt pity for the crowds because "they were skinned and thrown about like sheep without a shepherd." (Matthew 9:36) Doubtless this brought sorrow to him. When he went to the tomb of his friend Lazarus, who had just died, "Jesus gave way to tears."—John 11:35.

[31] So, just as we have, Jesus had occasions for sorrow. But did he let this destroy his happiness in knowing he was doing the work of his Father? Did he not exhibit joy in the disciples whom he taught and associated with for three years? There is no evidence that he went about with a mournful, negative spirit toward them or in their presence. Neither did he weaken or waver in faith or action. He knew that "in his hand what is the delight of Jehovah [would] succeed," and that he would receive from his Father "the keys of death and of Hades" and in time would therewith undo all the harm that sin and death bring about. —Isaiah 53:10; Revelation 1:18; 20:13.

[32] All these things give us a glimpse of the goodness of God. It moves our hearts to imitate him. And the wonderful thing about imitating him is that we can undergo grief in this present

---

30. What especially saddened Jesus?
31. How did Jesus, despite many saddening things, show that he never lost his joy?
32. (a) What can we conclude from our consideration of God's gifts? (b) How can we, in turn, bring gladness to God? (Psalm 149:4)

time and yet be happy. Moreover, by our obedience to him we can bring gladness to Jehovah himself. (Psalm 149:4; Proverbs 27:11) We can also know that there is a life to come when "neither will mourning nor outcry nor pain be anymore."—Revelation 21:4.

Chapter 9

Universal Law Reveals Purpose in Life

PEOPLE, both young and old, often incline to look upon any control of their lives as undesirable. But does resentment or resistance to any regulation of our actions really lead to happiness? Or, instead, can our enjoyment of personal freedom actually be enhanced by our submitting to certain regulations, and working in willing harmony with them—particularly those established by our Creator?

² The benefits of laws to our enjoyment of life can be seen in certain guiding or binding forces in the universe, often called "laws." One of these is the law of gravity. Such laws governing physical things are inescapable. We cannot ignore them or cancel them out. We cannot violate them with impunity. The penalty for violating such laws is usually executed immediately, as when, for example, someone jumps from a tall building.

---

1. How do people often view law?
2. What laws can we not evade, and yet how are these beneficial?

³ The physical laws are also constant, stable. If we could not predict how they would act from day to day, we could get very little work done. If we could not count on the sun's rising every day or rely on the seasons following one another in a certain order, we could tend to lose our sanity. Without constancy in the natural laws, living would be extremely difficult.

⁴ Take, for example, some substances with which we are familiar in everyday life. Consider oxygen, a gas that we must breathe in order to live. In its normal state it is indispensable to human and animal life. But three atoms of oxygen combine to make ozone, which is poisonous. However, it requires special conditions to produce ozone in the atmosphere. It does not happen accidentally, or just at any time in any place. The action of atoms of oxygen, as of all substances, is governed by strict laws preventing such accidental changes. Therefore we are not in fear of every breath we take, worried that our oxygen may have turned into ozone.

⁵ Where there is enforced law, there must be order. A law is not a passing chance occurrence, but refers to that which is continuous, steady. And when we see that this stability exists in the laws governing physical things, we know that there is a purpose in them. It helps us to realize that the Creator has a purpose in everything. God would also have to uphold and be personally involved in sustaining those laws. He could not

---

3. How is it to our benefit that the physical laws are stable, reliable?
4. Give an example of a substance that is governed by strict laws, and show how this is for our benefit.
5. What does the existence of the physical laws reveal to us about the Creator?

be one who is "far off," or who is not actually concerned with his universe. —Acts 17:27.

Astronauts traveling to the moon showed faith in laws governing speed, gravity and the orbits of the earth and the moon

6 The universal laws merit full confidence. When the astronauts traveled to the moon, they relied on the laws governing gravitation and on the precise speed and timing of earth and moon in their orbits. They *knew* that these laws would operate dependably and with exactness. The very slightest deviation would mean that the astronauts would be whirled out into space forever. They depended also on the principles of radio transmission and a host of other laws. They had confidence—actually *faith*—in the sureness of these laws. Really, *they staked their lives on that faith.* Their success is an outstanding testimony to universal law. Does not the fact that the heavenly bodies continue to move orderly and on time, without confusion or collision, imply that their Lawmaker is purposefully maintaining them? —Isaiah 40:26.

6. (a) Explain how scientists actually have faith in the physical laws governing the universe. (b) In what greater thing should their knowledge of the reliability of these laws bring faith?

PURPOSE MANIFEST
IN THE LAW OF PROCREATION

[7] Goodness and wisdom are evident in the physical laws and in the way that they work out in living things. Goodness can come only from intelligent purpose. A very impressive example of this is seen in God's law of procreation. How is this?

[8] Adam and Eve came on the earthly scene about 6,000 years ago, according to Bible history. They broke God's law—sinned, and passed on genetic defects to their children. These defects multiplied in succeeding generations. Each generation has added to these imperfections, multitudes doing everything imaginable that has damaged their bodies. Many have become drunkards, drug addicts and full of disease through immorality. Bad thinking, hatred and murder have also had their damaging effects.

[9] Yet, although no one is perfect, the great majority of babies born today are in a comparatively sound condition. They have two eyes,

7. Can a person see invisible qualities by observing the physical laws? (Romans 1:20)
8, 9. (a) How is goodness evident in God's law of procreation? (b) In what promise of God should this fact give us faith?

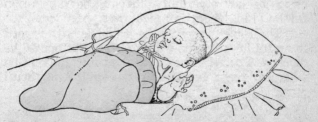

Despite thousands of years of human imperfection, God's laws still cause most babies to be normal at birth

two arms, two legs, possess all their faculties and
can live what we call "normal" lives. In view of
all the adverse forces operating for millenniums
in the human race, this is little short of miraculous—an evidence of the Creator's love and care
for humankind, as well as the fine quality and
sturdiness of his work. Since he was so careful
to arrange for the continuance of the human race
even though they brought bad conditions upon
themselves, should we not believe him when he
promises to give everlasting life, with perfect
conditions?

MORAL LAWS—VITAL TO PURPOSEFUL LIVING

[10] To his intelligent creatures God has given
another set of regulations—the moral laws. These
reflect God's purpose to an even greater degree.
In fact, a purpose is often expressly stated in
connection with God's moral laws. (For examples
read Deuteronomy 5:16, 33; Matthew 19:17;
Psalm 19:7-11; 1 Timothy 4:8.)

[11] The moral laws are as stable and as certain
in their outworking as are the laws governing
inanimate or unintelligent things. One who breaks
the moral laws cannot 'get away with it.' These
regulations are just as sure of being carried out
as is the law of gravity, though the retribution
for breaking them is not always so sudden.

[12] The Bible expresses the principle with regard
to moral laws in this way: "God is not one to be
mocked. For whatever a man is sowing, this he
will also reap; because he who is sowing with

---

10. What other laws must we consider to get a full understanding of God and his purpose?
11. Are the moral laws any more changeable or escapable
than the physical laws?
12. What does the Bible say as to the moral laws of God being
sure of enforcement?

a view to his flesh will reap corruption from his flesh, but he who is sowing with a view to the spirit will reap everlasting life from the spirit." —Galatians 6:7, 8.

¹³ By "flesh" the apostle meant the desires of the imperfect fleshly body. (Ephesians 2:3) By "spirit" he meant the spirit or active force of God that serves to guide His servants in a wholesome way. Paul illustrates the operation of these forces at Galatians 5:19-23:

> ¹⁴ "Now the works of the *flesh* are manifest, and they are fornication, uncleanness, loose conduct, idolatry, practice of spiritism, enmities, strife, jealousy, fits of anger, contentions, divisions, sects, envies, drunken bouts, revelries, and things like these. . . . On the other hand, the fruitage of the *spirit* is love, joy, peace, long-suffering, kindness, goodness, faith, mildness, self-control. Against such things there is no law."

RECOMPENSE FOR 'SOWING TO THE FLESH'

¹⁵ As testimony to the truth that God's moral laws cannot be ignored, the apostle Paul calls attention to what mankind has done. He comments that men had full opportunity, from observing God's creative works, to seek to learn more about him and to serve him. But, in the main, they rejected him and served gods of their own making. Paul continues:

> ¹⁶ "Therefore God, in keeping with the desires of their hearts, gave them up to uncleanness, that their bodies might be dishonored among them . . . That is why God gave them up to disgraceful sexual appetites, for both their females changed

13, 14. Explain what the apostle Paul meant when he spoke of 'sowing to the flesh' and 'sowing to the spirit.'
15, 16. How does the apostle Paul show the results to mankind in general for violating God's moral laws?

the natural use of themselves into one contrary to nature; and likewise even the males left the natural use of the female and became violently inflamed in their lust toward one another, males with males, working what is obscene and receiving in themselves the full recompense, which was due for their error."—Romans 1:24-27.

[17] This "recompense" consisted in many diseases, particularly venereal diseases. But also, such turning away from what is right resulted in mental difficulties and every sort of badness. Giving more details of the "recompense," Paul goes on to say:

[18] "And just as they did not approve of holding God in accurate knowledge, God gave them up to a disapproved mental state, to do the things not fitting, filled as they were with all unrighteousness, wickedness, covetousness, badness, being full of envy, murder, strife, deceit, malicious disposition, being whisperers, backbiters, haters of God, insolent, haughty, self-assuming, inventors of injurious things, disobedient to parents, without understanding, false to agreements, having no natural affection, merciless."—Romans 1:28-31.

[19] Such 'sowing to the flesh' has been a major cause of mankind's sad history. But in our time we see the works of the flesh causing greater distress than ever before, on a worldwide scale. Racial and nationalistic hatreds, hypocrisy, immorality, dishonesty, drug abuse, crime, vandalism and terrorism have brought about great fear and unhappiness in the earth. According to the Bible, such widespread, flagrant flouting of God's

17, 18. Besides physical diseases, what other troubles have mankind brought upon themselves by violating God's laws?
19, 20. What are some conditions in the earth today that give evidence that this present wicked system of things is near its end?

moral laws is evidence that this system of things is in its last days. We read:

> [20] "Know this, that in the last days critical times hard to deal with will be here. For men will be lovers of themselves, lovers of money, self-assuming, haughty, blasphemers, disobedient to parents, unthankful, disloyal, having no natural affection, not open to any agreement, slanderers, without self-control, fierce, without love of goodness, betrayers, headstrong, puffed up with pride, lovers of pleasures rather than lovers of God, having a form of godly devotion but proving false to its power; and from these turn away."—2 Timothy 3:1-5.

RELIGIOUS HYPOCRISY

[21] The latter part of the apostle's statement shows that it should be no cause for surprise to see the most reprehensible form of hypocrisy today—persons claiming to be servants of God, but proving false to their claim. Though they have a form of godly devotion, it is hollow. They do not believe that godliness will bring the real riches—spirituality, life and peace. Really, it is not the kind of gain that they want. Their "form of godly devotion" is a false front so that they may give a "holy" appearance to a selfish, immoral course of life. As God's Word says: "They publicly declare they know God, but they disown him by their works, because they are detestable and disobedient and not approved for good work of any sort."—Titus 1:16.

[22] Jesus Christ had trouble with such men among the religious leaders of the Jews. He said to them: "You hypocrites, Isaiah aptly prophesied

21. What fulfillment do we see today of the apostle's words at 2 Timothy 3:5?
22. Who were the men that gave Jesus the greatest trouble when he was on earth, and why did he warn the people not to follow their practices?

about you, when he said, 'This people honors me
with their lips, yet their heart is far removed from
me. It is in vain that they keep worshiping me,
because they teach commands of men as doctrines.' " (Matthew 15:7-9) He warned the people
to take care not to practice their righteousness
in front of men merely in order to be observed
by them. He said that the hypocrites performed
their acts of "mercy" in the synagogues and in
the streets, 'that they might be glorified by men.'
—Matthew 6:1, 2.

²³ Speaking of the day when he would act as
judge of mankind, Jesus said: "Many will say to
me in that day, 'Lord, Lord, did we not prophesy
in your name, and expel demons in your name,
and perform many powerful works in your name?'
And yet then I will confess to them: I never knew
you! Get away from me, you workers of lawlessness."—Matthew 7:22, 23.

²⁴ From Jesus' words we see that Jehovah the
Universal Lawmaker is going to see that his laws
are carried out. He also purposes to bring all
intelligent creation into full harmony with his
moral laws, so that there will no longer be viola-
tions. This will require an adverse judgment for
persistent, irreformable lawbreakers. (1 Peter
4:17, 18) It will also call for a merciful consideration of others who have violated moral laws.
(Psalm 103:8-10) Who would these be? Persons
who have sinned through ignorance, imperfections
and weaknesses. There is also a worldly spirit
that, much like a mob spirit, motivates people to

23. Do we have any counterpart of those religious men in our
time, when judgment is near?
24. (a) Will there be a time when God's laws will no longer
be violated? (b) What people will receive adverse judgment
and who will receive mercy?

violate laws of honesty and morality. (Ephesians 2:1-3) Persons who have been swept up with such spirit may later regret this and be shown mercy by God.—Luke 19:8-10; Acts 7:57-60; 1 Corinthians 15:9.

25 Can we confidently count on such just, yet merciful, treatment? Yes, because the whole structure of God's law, both physical and moral, is actually for the final purpose of benefiting, not condemning, mankind.

26 Is it not time, therefore, for the honest-hearted people of earth to look to the Universal Lawgiver, to get back into harmony with him? Obedience to his laws is not burdensome but brings freedom—the very reverse of what we see today.—1 John 5:3; 2 Corinthians 3:17.

27 Accordingly, anyone loving life in peace and security should take these things seriously to heart and make immediate adjustments in his life. He should bring it as fully as possible into harmony with God's laws. Jehovah admonished the nation of Israel: "Come, now, you people, and let us set matters straight between us . . . Though the sins of you people should prove to be as scarlet, they will be made white just like snow."—Isaiah 1:18.

28 Someone may ask: 'But can I set matters straight with God? Would Jehovah God care for me and deal with me as an *individual*? Perhaps I am too bad for him to listen to me.' Whether God is interested in *you* is the subject for our investigation in the following chapter.

25, 26. Why is it reasonable and timely to get back into harmony with the Creator?
27. What can a person who loves life and peace do to have peace and favor from God?
28. What important questions now merit our consideration?

Chapter 10

Does God Count You Personally Important?

HOW does God view humankind? As just a mass of persons, or as individuals? Or does he bestow his favor upon a selected and certain group and ignore the rest?

² To God, every person is important as a distinct individual. (Acts 17:26, 27) He "desires all men to be saved and to come to the knowledge of the truth." (1 Timothy 2: 4, *Revised Standard Version*) The apostle Peter, see-

Does God view humans simply as a mass of faces? . . .

1, 2. How do we know that God does not view people as a mere "faceless" mass, but is interested in every individual?

108

ing God's acceptance of Gentiles into the Christian congregation, exclaimed: "For a certainty I perceive that God is not partial, but in every nation the man [the individual person] that fears him and works righteousness is acceptable to him." —Acts 10:34, 35; 15:8, 9.

³ Jesus Christ was sent by God to give himself "a corresponding ransom for all." (1 Timothy 2:6) He 'tasted death for *every man.*' (Hebrews 2:9) Would it then be logical for God's Son to have an unconcerned attitude, saying, in effect: 'I gave my lifeblood for everyone, but of what importance is this one person? Whether he loses his life or not makes no difference to me'? Never! Each individual will receive attention, with opportunity for life.

⁴ Because of Jesus' ransom sacrifice, he is mankind's "repurchaser." Jehovah God, by reason of his Creatorship, owns the human race. But as children of rebellious Adam, they have been "sold under sin," as "slaves of sin." (Romans 7:14; 6:16, 17) As such they need to be reconciled or

. . . Or is God interested in us as individuals?

3. How did Jesus Christ demonstrate that he has the same consideration for every individual as does his Father?

4. What position does Jesus Christ occupy as to the human race, and how did he receive this position?

brought back into good relationship with God. (Romans 5:10) In order to help them, Jesus had to buy them, to become their new family head or father, the "last Adam," because the first Adam did the selling of them into sin. (1 Corinthians 15:45) This legal transaction was foreshadowed in the law of Moses, at Leviticus 25:47-49.

⁵ Accordingly, God has given Jesus Christ "authority to do judging, because Son of man he is." (John 5:27) That is, becoming a human on earth in the likeness of men but without sin, Jesus became their near relative with the right and the price to repurchase mankind. (Philippians 2:7; Romans 8:3) His title "Son of man" denotes this. (Hebrews 2:11, 14, 15) As a wholly just judge, he does not slight anyone. He said: "The judgment that I render is righteous, because I seek, not my own will, but the will of him that sent me." (John 5:30) Therefore he does not judge according to outward appearance nor does he judge people 'en masse,' but according to each person's own circumstances and attitude.—Isaiah 11:3, 4; Hebrews 4:15.

⁶ God's dealings, particularly his use of Jesus Christ, reveal that he wants all people to come into a position that will enable them to receive his blessing. This includes wrongdoers as individuals. The apostle Paul wrote to those who were practicing wrong things: "Do you despise the riches of his kindness and forbearance and long-suffering, because you do not know that the kindly quality of God is trying to lead you to

---

5. (a) How did Jesus come to have "authority to do judging"? (b) What kind of judgment does he render?
6. How do the apostles Paul and Peter emphasize the individualness of God's dealings?

repentance? . . . And he will render to *each one* according to his works." Also, the apostle Peter called attention to the individualness of God's dealings when he referred to Him as "the Father who judges impartially according to *each one's work.*"—Romans 2:4-6; 1 Peter 1:17.

OPPORTUNITY FOR EVERYONE

[7] However, someone may say: 'There is no use for me to try now to serve God. I am so bad that I can't be recovered. There's no hope for me.' It is a serious mistake to think that way. Of course, no one is worthy, on his own merit, of any consideration from God. (Romans 5:6-10) If perfection were required, everyone would be eliminated. But through his kindness, God has recorded examples to show that he will not reject any repentant person, regardless of his past bad works. He requires only that the person be willing to learn what to do and make sincere effort to come into harmony with Him.—Isaiah 1:18; Revelation 22:17.

[8] The apostle Paul was such an example. He was formerly involved in the actual *murder* of Christians. (Acts 7:58, 59; 9:1, 2) Paul himself says: "Faithful and deserving of full acceptance is the saying that Christ Jesus came into the world to save sinners. *Of these I am foremost.* Nevertheless, the reason why I was shown mercy was that by means of me as the foremost case

---

7. Why is it the wrong viewpoint for a person to say he is too bad to be recovered and to become a servant of God?
8-10. (a) Give two examples that are comforting to persons who have done wrong but who want to turn to God. (b) How do Ezekiel 33:14-16 and Colossians 3:5-8 show that what counts with God is what we are doing now, not what we have done in the past?

Christ Jesus might demonstrate all his long-suffering for a sample of those who are going to rest their faith on him for everlasting life."
—1 Timothy 1:15, 16.

⁹ King Manasseh of Judah was another example of a very bad man. He took the lead in bringing the nation into extreme idolatry and rebelliousness against God. The nation never recovered. (2 Kings 21:11, 16) But Manasseh himself, in later times, repented and his prayer was accepted by God.
—2 Chronicles 33:11-13, 16, 17.

¹⁰ What a person is doing *now* and in the future, not what he or she has done in the past, is what counts with God.—Ezekiel 33:14-16; Colossians 3:5-8.

¹¹ On the other hand, no person should think that by his own goodness or righteous acts he will receive God's favor. (Romans 3:10) He would thereby be denying the fact that he is a sinner. (1 John 1:8-10) Such a misled individual is rejecting Christ's sacrifice as unnecessary. It is an attempt to be self-righteous by works—to 'obligate' God to accept him because of his own personal 'goodness.' (Romans 4:2-8) Persons who have this attitude are not really serving God, but are setting their own standard in place of God's. The futility of this effort was proved by the Jews who tried to get righteousness through the Mosaic law.—Romans 10:1-3; Hebrews 10:1, 2.

¹² Nor does God favor only a certain class of people. Did not his Son, Jesus, have a feeling for *all?* Or did he, for example, use his healing power

---

11. Can a person, by his own righteousness, or by living up to the Ten Commandments or the Mosaic law, earn God's favor and life?
12. How did Jesus demonstrate that God does not show partiality, or help only those with money or position?

only on his favorites, or on those who could give him money? No, there are many accounts of crowds of people coming to him with all forms of sickness, and he cured them *all*.—Matthew 14:14.

JEHOVAH'S 'ATTACHMENT' TO THOSE SERVING HIM

¹³ Jehovah is always willing to grant his help and his love to anyone who will receive it. And the intensity and constancy of his love are far greater than we are able to express toward others. Note God's love for Abraham, Isaac and Jacob, who were imperfect men but who served him wholeheartedly. *Centuries later* Moses told the nation of Israel: "To your forefathers did Jehovah get *attached* so as to love them." (Deuteronomy 10:15) He put up with the nation's stubbornness for centuries because of this love.—Deuteronomy 7:7, 8.

¹⁴ Jehovah's love is just as great and lasting for those who serve him today. (Romans 8:38, 39) He is, so to speak, watching for an opportunity to "get attached" to anyone who calls on him in sincerity and truth. (James 4:8) "As regards Jehovah," says the Bible, "his eyes are roving about through all the earth to show his strength in behalf of those whose heart is complete toward him." (2 Chronicles 16:9) "His ears are toward their supplication."—1 Peter 3:12.

¹⁵ As Jehovah views the earth and sees the many distresses that men undergo, he has a deep feeling for humankind. His desire is to help them.

---

13. What examples do we have in Abraham and others of the intensity and constancy of God's love?
14. Can an individual who calls on God in sincerity and truth confidently expect God's help?
15. As Jehovah God views us, what is he looking for?

Though he does not 'turn a blind eye' to wrong-doing, he is not looking for people's faults, but for their good points. (Psalm 130:3) He 'remembers that they are dust.'—Psalm 103:14.

¹⁶ When on earth, God's Son was anxious to use his power to help people. When a leper said to him: "If you just want to, you can make me clean," Jesus "was moved with pity, and he stretched out his hand and touched him, and said to him: *I want to.* Be made clean,'" and so he cured him.—Mark 1:40, 41.

¹⁷ Jesus' healing of people who came to him for help was accompanied by deep feeling. In the same way God and his Son are at this time showing concern and love to anyone who has paused in the affairs of everyday life to give consideration to the good news about God's purpose. Are you right now looking into God's Word in a genuinely searching way to find out more about him? If so, this in itself is a proof that he is interested in you. How can this be said with assurance?

WE MUST HAVE GOD'S HELP TO UNDERSTAND

¹⁸ This statement is true because God sees some goodness of heart in anyone sincerely inquiring into his Word. As a result, he opens that one's mind to understanding. Jesus said: "No man can come to me unless the Father, who sent me, draws him." (John 6:44) You cannot understand the purposes of God without the help of God's

16, 17. (a) How did Jesus show that he really wanted to help people? (b) How do Jehovah and his Son feel toward people today?

18, 19. (a) If a person sincerely inquires into God's Word, how will he receive help? (b) Why do we need the help of God's spirit?

spirit, his invisible active force, which can influence and direct your mind.

[19] The apostle Paul wrote: "No one has come to know the things of God, except the spirit of God. [That is, God's spirit is essential for transmitting God's thoughts and purposes to us.] Now we received, not the spirit of the world, but the spirit which is from God, that we might know the things that have been kindly given us by God." (1 Corinthians 2:11, 12; compare Acts 16:14.) If you did not have this help, then the confusion of this world, its lack of faith and its spirit, which is in opposition to God, would overcome you, for "faith is not a possession of all people."—1 Corinthians 2:14; 2 Thessalonians 3:2.

[20] In this responding to your effort to get understanding, God is displaying another fine quality toward you. That quality is *appreciation*. You no doubt have and express appreciation for good things that others do for you. But the appreciation that humans feel is far less deep and heartfelt than God's appreciation of those who show faith in him and who have respect for his Word. He *rejoices* in them. Jesus even spoke about joy in heaven over one sinner that repents or forsakes wrong things in order to please God. (Luke 15:10) Why, Jesus said that a person giving just a cup of cold water to one whom he recognized to be a servant of God would by no means fail to be rewarded. (Matthew 10:42) God observes and appreciates each one who respects his name and treats his people kindly. So, his heart and his help go out to that person.—Consider the example recorded at Mark 14:3-9.

20. How deep is God's appreciation of the person who is diligently trying to learn of and serve him?

²¹ We, in turn, should rightly show appreciation for God's kindness in helping us to know about his purpose and in giving us the opportunity to get everlasting life. A person should be thankful that God has seen fit to allow him to be like the people to whom Paul preached in one city in Asia Minor. There the Jews, who claimed to serve God, opposed the truth. But the record states: "When those of the nations [Gentiles] heard [of the opportunity to be accepted by God], they began to rejoice and to glorify the word of Jehovah, and all those who were rightly disposed for everlasting life became believers." (Acts 13:48) Those people appreciated God's kindness. This appreciation helped them to be the kind of people God is pleased to accept.

RESURRECTION, A PROOF OF GOD'S INTEREST

²² A strong proof of God's interest in every individual is his provision of a resurrection for "the righteous and the unrighteous." (Acts 24:15) In order to resurrect a person, God has to know *everything* about him. Only with this information can God bring back the same person with the same personality, so that the individual will be *himself* and recognize himself. This means that God must restore every detail of the person's makeup. This would include his appearance, his inherited traits, the influence that environment and experience have had on him, along with his complete memory. What interest and care this demonstrates!

21. How did certain Gentile persons in Asia Minor show what our response should be to God's kindness?
22. How does Jehovah's provision of a resurrection show that he has a very deep interest in individuals?

Men can make films that preserve the actions and voice of a person long after his death. God remembers even more, and he can resurrect the dead

²³ Someone may say, 'That seems impossible.' But even today men can make a videotape or moving picture of a person. Then, even after he is dead, they can project it on a screen and see the actions and movements of the individual, along with hearing his voice. Hundreds of details are recorded. If men can do this, cannot God, with whom "all things are possible," have a record of the thousands of details that make up a personality?—Matthew 19:26; Job 42:2.

²⁴ Even we, as imperfect humans, know many

23, 24. (a) What remarkable record of a person can puny men make that helps us to see how easily God could resurrect an individual? (b) What about his remembering and resurrecting people who have been dead for thousands of years?

details about a close friend so that we can describe him with fair accuracy. Yet, with the passage of time the image grows dim. God, with his far greater insight, knows *completely* every detail of all persons. He knows what is in the hearts of all. (Hebrews 4:13) Moreover, even if one is dead for centuries, God's memory of that person does not fade.—Job 14:13-15.

[25] Consequently, the billions of people in the grave are yet in God's mind in clear detail. (Proverbs 15:11) Even those who have not been buried, but who have been destroyed in the sea, or by burning and otherwise, are just as vividly in his memory.—Revelation 20:13.

[26] As to those whom God purposes to resurrect, Jesus said: "He is a God, not of the dead, but of the living, for they are all living to him." (Luke 20:38) His power and wisdom make his purposes so certain that he "makes the dead alive and calls the things that are not as though they were." —Romans 4:17.

[27] God has given Jesus Christ the power to perform the resurrection. When on earth, he demonstrated this power in several instances. —Luke 7:14, 15; 8:49-56; John 11:39, 43, 44.

[28] Could anyone rightly say, then, that God and his Son are not interested in him? Do such

---

25. Does the resurrection include people who have not been buried in a grave, but have been lost at sea, eaten by animals, and so forth?

26. What did Jesus mean when he spoke about Jehovah as 'the God of Abraham, Isaac and Jacob,' and then said: "He is a God, not of the dead, but of the living, for they are all living to him"? (Luke 20:37, 38)

27. How can we be sure that Christ has been given the authority and power to resurrect the dead?

28. (a) How can we respond with appreciation to the things Jehovah has done for us? (b) Should any normal person feel that he is mentally incapable of learning Jehovah's purposes from the Bible?

care and interest on Jehovah's part find a response in your heart? You can express appreciation to him by learning more about him and by encouraging others to do so. And your learning about him will be in proportion to the sincere effort you put forth in getting knowledge of him. He will supply you with the "intellectual capacity" to do so.—1 John 5:20.

Chapter 11

You Can Know God's Purpose

WE OFTEN hear the question, 'What is truth?' or, 'How can a person know that he has the truth?' Is it possible to know with certainty the purpose of God toward humankind?—John 18:38.

² Jesus answered these questions when he said: "If you remain in my word, you are really my disciples, and you will know the truth, and the truth will set you free."—John 8:31, 32.

³ Jesus knew without any doubt that he had the truth, because he had been with Jehovah God before coming to the earth. (John 3:13; 17:5) The apostles, in turn, knew that they had the truth, because they learned it from Jesus, and from the Hebrew Scriptures, which Jesus acknowledged as the truth from God. Furthermore, what Jesus said and did fulfilled many of the Hebrew Scripture prophecies. These Scriptures, commonly

1-4. How can we know what is the truth?

called the "Old Testament," had been given to the nation of Israel by God through inspiration of his servants.

⁴ We now have the entire Bible. It contains both the Hebrew Scriptures (often called the "Old Testament") and the Greek Scriptures (the so-called "New Testament")—the writings of the apostles and their close associates.

WRITTEN RECORD MORE HELPFUL

⁵ But, why a *book?* Why not a direct communication by God's voice, or through angels sent by him?

⁶ It is true that God at first did communicate by word of mouth to Adam, instructing him. But he has since used other means just as effective, and, for imperfect persons, even more appropriate. Really, because of the defective memories of all humans, it is good that God has had his communications written down since the time of Adam.

⁷ Consider the wisdom of God in causing his communication to mankind to be available in written form. Certainly this is a more reliable record than a mere spoken word would be. Passing on information by word of mouth from person to person would be a very inaccurate method. God would need to repeat all his instructions to every generation. And if God had a message for all mankind, he would have to speak to certain men as his representatives or prophets, who would then transmit it to others. Otherwise he would have to speak to all people in fearful, thundering tones from heaven. Though very impressive, this

5-7. How did God communicate with man at first, but why is it good that God's communications have been written down?

could have undesirable effects, as Exodus 20:18, 19 shows.

⁸ However, in the Bible we have "all the counsel of God" for everyone to read. (Acts 20:27) Nothing needs to be added or subtracted. (Proverbs 30:5, 6) The principles governing mankind are the same at all times and places. And, having all of God's communication to us provided in a book, any part of it can conveniently be referred to at will for consultation on any human problem.

⁹ Also, we must keep in mind that the Bible contains, not only God's counsel, but also history and accounts of individual lives of those serving God and those not serving him. We see the outcome of their lives. The Bible gives us an account of God's dealings with humankind, so that we know how he feels about certain matters. (Romans 15:4) Out of the thousands of events of history, God chose certain events to be recorded, to illustrate principles. Some events were prophetic. (Galatians 4:24) Some were examples taken from real life that serve for our guidance today.—1 Corinthians 10:11.

¹⁰ Since we have and need these accounts for proper guidance, is it not good that they were written by real people, about real people, often themselves? And they were very honest and candid, not hiding their mistakes and sins. Does it not reach the heart to read about the experiences, hardships, joys, courage and faith of real people? Such things appeal to the heart and to the conscience far better than would a book

8. Does the Bible contain all of God's counsel for us today? How?
9. What benefit do we get from the historical record in the Bible?
10. How does the fact that men were used to write the Bible help us to understand and to be moved to act in faith?

of rules. You can picture in your mind the events recorded in the Bible as occurring; in fact, you can even identify yourself personally with them. When we read the real-life experiences of Moses, David, Jeremiah and Paul, do we not have a warm feeling? And these accounts have the ring of truth. Are you not moved because of the reality and forcefulness of these written accounts?—Compare Jeremiah 20:8-11; Acts 23:12-24.

AUTHENTIC, THOUGH WRITTEN BY MEN

[11] True, God transmitted his message to us by the hand of imperfect men. But there is no reason to think that the Bible is any less authentic than would be a message from God by word of mouth, through angels, or through a book written in heaven and dropped to earth. And it has far more human appeal. The proof of the Bible's appeal is that it is by far the most widely distributed book, translated into many more languages than any other book. It is the most enduring, and has given guidance to men and women of all ages and in all places.

[12] God is not a liar. (Numbers 23:19) In getting a message to the human race he would certainly see that it contained no lie. The vision of the "transfiguration" is an instance where a vision from God, along with God's words, corroborated the authenticity of "Old Testament" events and characters.—Matthew 17:1-9.

[13] The methods used in transmitting the written information that we have in the Bible were varied. But God was always directly involved. He himself wrote the basic laws of the covenant with Israel,

11, 12. Though the Bible was written by imperfect men, how can we be assured that it is authentic and correct?
13. How did God oversee the writing of the Bible?

the Ten Commandments. (Exodus 31:18; Deuteronomy 10:1-4) God spoke "mouth to mouth" with Moses, who wrote down word for word much of what he heard. (Numbers 12:8) The tabernacle pattern was shown to Moses in a vision. (Exodus 25:9; Numbers 8:4) Then, angels at times brought direct messages from God. (Genesis 19:1; Judges 6:12, 21; Luke 1:26-28) Prophets had visions and God-directed dreams. (Genesis 46:2; Daniel 1:17) Other writers were guided in their expression by God's invisible active force, his spirit.—2 Samuel 23:2; 2 Timothy 3:16, 17; 2 Peter 1:20, 21.

[14] Furthermore, we have the recorded words and acts of Jesus Christ, who came forth as a direct representative of Jehovah God. He revealed Jehovah perfectly. (John 16:27, 28) So well did he portray the thinking and ways of his Father in every respect that he could say: "He that has seen me has seen the Father also." (John 14:9) The account of Jesus' life is in the Bible so that we can see how he spoke and acted. Could we have any better communication than this?—Hebrews 1:1, 2.

COMPILATION OF THE BIBLE GUARDED

[15] It is easy for God to accomplish his full objective in the way that he sees fit. (Isaiah 46:10) Since he inspired the writing of the Scriptures it is logical that he would cause faithful men to gather together the Hebrew Scriptures as being authentically from God. These are the books that the Jewish nation recognized for centuries as God's communication to them. And our con-

14. What further strong evidence do we have that we really can know Jehovah's ways?
15, 16. What evidence do we have that the present-day Bible contains the whole counsel of God for his people?

fidence that their selection was divinely guided, and not the result of human preference, is fortified when we realize that these very books frequently condemned the nation for its disobedient ways.

[16] Then the early Christians, guided by the same spirit of God, selected and catalogued the inspired writings of the apostles and their associates. These writings have been significant for the instruction of Christians throughout the past nineteen centuries.

[17] So we do not need to wait for a voice out of the heavens, or for even another book in order to know God's purpose. The Bible gives the only reliable history of mankind from the beginning. Search the religious books of the world and you will not find all these things that are found in the Bible, namely: A realistic and reasonable account of creation, why mankind dies, a genealogical and chronological account of mankind from Adam onward, the way of deliverance from sin and death, the purpose of God toward man and the earth, and the principles to live by to attain eternal life. Added to this are the prophecies, those that have been fulfilled and those yet to be fulfilled with the happy conclusion of an everlasting reign of peace on earth.

[18] Thousands of years have passed since Bible writing began. What, then, about the Bible as we have it today? Of course, the original autographed manuscripts by the Bible writers are not available. But there are many copies in the original languages. The original Bible languages are Hebrew and Greek, with some Aramaic sections

17. What credentials does the Bible have as God's book?
18-22. Since many copies of the original writings have been made, are there not many errors, making the present-day Bible unreliable? Explain.

and words. We can have faith that the God who inspired the Bible would guard its being copied, so that a person reading the Bible would not be misled because of serious errors in it. What do scholars say, those who have studied the hundreds of original-language manuscripts available?

[19] Sir Frederic Kenyon, Bible scholar and former director of the British Museum, stated, in the introduction to his seven volumes on the "Chester Beatty Biblical Papyri" (which were very ancient Greek manuscripts of portions of the "New Testament"):

> [20] "The first and most important conclusion derived from the examination of [the Papyri] is the satisfactory one that they confirm the essential soundness of the existing texts. No striking or fundamental variation is shown either in the Old or the New Testament. There are no important omissions or additions of passages, and no variations which affect vital facts or doctrines. The variations of text affect minor matters, such as the order of words or the precise words used . . . But their essential importance is their confirmation, by evidence of an earlier date than was hitherto available, of the integrity of our existing texts. In this respect they are an acquisition of epoch-making value."

[21] This scholar also said concerning the "New Testament":

> [22] "The last foundation for any doubt that the Scriptures have come down to us substantially as they were written has now been removed. Both the *authenticity* and the *general integrity* of the books of the New Testament may be regarded as finally established."

[23] Today, in translations of the Bible into modern-day languages, we have the products of

_____

23. Of what advantage are the various Bible translations that are available today?

much careful study of the Scripture writings by scholars who have devoted their lives to this study. Most translations are the result of comparisons of Hebrew and Greek manuscripts and are carefully edited. They can provide a good understanding of God's purposes. If the meaning of a certain text is not quite clear to you, you can compare several translations in your own language, which usually vary slightly in a few places, mainly in word choice. In this way you can get the flavor of the original Hebrew and Greek expressions, and may come to an even more precise understanding.

THE BIBLE, A COMPLETE GUIDE

[24] There are some people who read Bible accounts and complain, 'If this is God's Word and a guide for us, why are there so few details in some of the accounts?' They point to the brevity of the creation account, among others. The Bible itself answers that God has put into the Bible *what is sufficient,* all we really need. It says: "All Scripture is inspired of God and beneficial for teaching, for reproving, for setting things straight, for disciplining in righteousness, that the man of God may be *fully competent, completely equipped for every good work.*" (2 Timothy 3:16, 17) So the Bible is ample to "make you wise for salvation." (2 Timothy 3:15) It is "perfect" in this sense.

[25] Another point worthy of note: As God's word or message to mankind, the Bible is written in such a way that those who are not truly seeking God—who have no genuine faith in God—are induced to 'show their true colors.' For example,

24, 25. (a) Why does the Bible not give every detail of the things that took place? (b) So how is the Bible "perfect"?

it does not give every detail of every account it records. At times it describes God's action or judgment on a matter without explaining why he so judged. It lets two writers give their own observation of an event from different viewpoints.* It leaves those not wanting to serve God a 'way out,' an excuse to find fault, if this is their desire. In this way, too, the Bible is complete or perfect, for it fulfills a purpose of God in causing persons —both haughty ones and humble ones—to reveal what is in their hearts.—Hebrews 4:12; Matthew 13:34, 35; Luke 8:10.

COMMUNICATING WITH GOD

26 While bringing us God's message, the Bible points out for us, in turn, a way to communicate our inmost thoughts and heartfelt desires to God. This is by prayer. You need not fear that God will not listen to you. His only requirement is a sincere heart and acknowledgment that one is a sinner, needing help. (Psalms 119:145; 34:18) One who cries out to him will be shown what to do. Such a person will come to know that prayers addressed to God must be offered through Jesus Christ as God's appointed High Priest.—John 16:23, 24; Hebrews 4:15.

27 What are proper subjects for prayer? Anything that will affect one's relationship to God; anything that will affect one spiritually. The apostle John wrote: *"No matter what it is that we ask according to his will, he hears us."*—1 John 5:14.

---

* See *Is the Bible Really the Word of God?* (Chapter 7), published by Watchtower Bible and Tract Society of New York, Inc., 117 Adams St., Brooklyn, New York 11201.

26. Can we, in turn, communicate with God?
27. What are proper subjects for prayer? (Matthew 6:9-13)

[28] "According to his will" would mean that we rightly would not pray for things that promote strictly selfish interests, such as riches, position above our fellowman, revenge, selfish pleasures and like things. But we may, for example, petition God with regard to marriage—for his help in providing a suitable mate. Married couples may pray regarding the bearing of children, or for wisdom in rearing their children. (1 Samuel 1:10, 11, 17, 20; Judges 13:8-14) These things definitely affect our lives and require adjustments in which we need God's wisdom. God is interested in our personal problems. Even a move to another location or another job may be a subject for prayer, because one's family may be affected economically and spiritually. Whatever it is, the desire to find and to do *God's will* is the primary factor. Each person, of course, has his own circumstances, different from others, and this will affect the subjects of his prayers.

[29] The answer from God can be expected in the form of wise guidance in the person's own individual case. (Psalm 32:8) Of course, he should be consistent and act in harmony with his prayer. He should seek for counsel on the problem from the Bible. He may consult others who can help him to see what the Bible says on the matter. He should persist in praying on the matter until he gets a clear understanding of what is the wise course to take. (Luke 18:2-5) Having done so, no one else can rightly criticize him for decisions conscientiously made, because "to his own master [God] he stands or falls. Indeed, he will be made

28. (a) What is praying 'according to God's will'? (b) What are some personal things for which it is proper to pray?
29. How can a person receive the answer to his prayer about a certain matter?

to stand, for Jehovah can make him stand."
—Romans 14:4, 10, 12.

[30] The person who prays and acts with faith
in God can be assured that he will be guided so
as to take the most beneficial course. (Proverbs
3:5, 6) He will come really to *know* God, who
promises: "The intimacy with Jehovah belongs
to those fearful of him." (Psalm 25:14) This is
not a morbid fear, but a wholesome respect for
God, because if you love God you will want to
take your problems to him, and will have no fear
of being rebuffed or rejected. Of such inhibiting
fear, the apostle John says: "Perfect love throws
fear outside, because fear exercises a restraint."
(1 John 4:18) You should never be fearful or
hesitant to take the most intimate matters, *whatever they are,* to Jehovah—including your sins.
He will not view your problem as foolish or
laugh at you. "He gives generously to all and
without reproaching."—James 1:5; 1 John 1:9.

[31] Some may complain because they sometimes
face very bad or discouraging circumstances. They
may say, 'Why does God let such terrible conditions exist in the earth?' But should we overlook what God has done in giving the Bible to
his earthly creatures? If followed, that inspired
Word would enable all humankind to live a very
good life even under conditions of imperfection.
Think of how different things would be if people
would, for example, follow the rule: 'All things
that you want men to do to you, you also must
likewise do to them.' (Matthew 7:12) What a

30. (a) To what fine position will prayer bring us? (b) Why
should we not be afraid to take any matter or problem to God
in prayer?
31. How can an understanding of the Bible and obedience to
its principles help us to live a good and happier life now?

change this could bring on earth! And in God's new system of things all persons *will* be guided by such principles. That is one reason why this earth will then be such a desirable place in which to live.

[32] Jesus said: "Even though you do not believe me, believe the works [that I do], in order that you may come to know and may continue knowing that the Father is in union with me and I am in union with the Father." (John 10:38) If you have doubts as to the Bible's worth, you can see its value by observing the results in the lives of thousands of people who are making the Bible their guide. Therefore, we can have confidence that the Bible's promises of life for those who follow its guidance are sure of fulfillment.

---

32. To those who may have doubts about the Bible, what recommends it as a book to be studied?

Chapter 12

How Far Has Preparation Progressed?

MUCH has been said in our study thus far about God's purpose. But what has he been doing to bring that purpose to completion? Some people, not seeing world affairs getting better, say that "God is dead," meaning that he is not doing anything to help mankind.

[2] Such attitude results because it takes a measure

1, 2. (a) What do people usually mean by the expression, "God is dead"? (b) Why do some people say this?

of faith to see God's progressive preparation for a righteous new system of things that will govern the earth. "Faith," says the Bible, "is the assured expectation of things hoped for, the evident demonstration of realities though not beheld."—Hebrews 11:1.

³ The person without faith has no real expectation or hope regarding God because he does not believe what God promises. To such a person the things seen appear *on the surface* to be contrary to what the one with faith is looking for. But why does God require faith?

⁴ God is like a father who wants his children to love him for his goodness and to accept his promises, not having to *see* everything before they believe their father. A child who has no faith in a good father will also be disobedient and will eventually bring trouble and disgrace on the family. Such a child is undeserving of parental affection. But, just as a good father would do, God responds to his earthly creatures who look to him in faith, and he helps them.—Psalm 119:65-68.

⁵ An illustration of the deceptive surface appearance of things, as compared with the way that faith sees the true situation, is found in the destruction of Jerusalem in 70 C.E. About thirty-three years before it happened, Jesus foretold that a time would come when Jerusalem would be surrounded by armies. When that occurred, he said, Christians should immediately get out of the city, for Jerusalem's destruction would be near. (Luke 21:20-24) According to the first-

---

3. How do things appear to the person without faith?
4. Why does God require faith?
5, 6. (a) Illustrate how events may be very deceptive to those without faith. (b) What was the difference between the Christians and the majority of the Jews in 66-70 C.E.?

century Jewish historian Josephus, the Romans under General Cestius Gallus, in 66 C.E., surrounded Jerusalem, intending to take the city. Then, for some unexplained reason, Gallus withdrew. Those Jews and others who had become Christians immediately fled, because they recognized that this was exactly what Jesus had prophesied. Other Jews, however, pursued Gallus' troops and inflicted heavy casualties upon them.

⁶ The majority of Jerusalem's Jews were elated at their victory. The danger appeared past. But the Christians did not try to return to Jerusalem. This may have looked foolish to the Jews who had remained behind. However, less than four years later the Romans returned under General Titus and completely destroyed the city and more than nine tenths of its inhabitants. Yes, those having faith saw that which did not appear on the surface and saved their lives. They saw something that the Jews in general, though they had the opportunity to do so, did not see. As a people, the Jews had rejected Jesus Christ, and so had rejected the wisdom that would have saved them. —Compare Jeremiah 8:9.

⁷ We need to get the right perspective as to what God has been doing toward bringing about an end to mankind's suffering, just as he has promised. How can we do this? By examining the historical record. If we do, we will see that God has been progressively working out his purpose from the beginning of mankind's troubles. We will see, not just theories or speculations, but "the evident demonstration of realities" on which to build firm faith.

---

7. How can we know that God has been working toward the fulfillment of his promise?

LAYING A FOUNDATION

⁸ Jehovah has promised that he will govern the entire earth, bringing in peace and unity. But he is not going to rule simply by force. He purposes to have people enlightened, educated to know him and to submit willingly to his administration. (Psalm 110:3) With this in view, it has taken time to establish a foundation for an entire *world* of mankind that would serve him. God had to provide a knowledge of the standards and principles of his righteous administration and how it operates.

⁹ But Jehovah is an invisible God. (1 Timothy 1:17) How would he make men of flesh and blood understand? Not by a mere display of power, speaking in awe-inspiring tones from heaven. No, God would reveal his principles and qualities by having dealings with people. How much more instructive, convincing and moving, not only to hear and read God's declarations as recorded by faithful men, but, additionally, to see in the historical record the proof that what he said he also carried out.

¹⁰ For the first part of mankind's history—up to the time of the Flood—Jehovah God let men go the way they chose, either to put faith in him or not. But he demonstrated that he was no "dead" or inactive God when he destroyed that world. The reason was that it had become so corrupt that it endangered pure worship and the lives of those who wanted to do what was right. God preserved in the ark those few who at that

---

8. Why has God taken a long time to bring in his rule over earth?
9. Why is God's way of teaching us better than if he spoke in a loud voice from heaven?
10. When did God first strikingly demonstrate to the world that he is no inactive God, but is interested in men's affairs?

time acknowledged his rulership.—Genesis 6:11-13, 17-20; 1 Peter 3:20.

[11] After the Flood, God proceeded to lay a foundation for his coming administration of earth's affairs by the promised "seed," the Messiah. In the meantime, God let the nations go on in their independent course and make a record that stands as proof of men's inability to govern themselves.

[12] In laying the foundation for his government over the earth, Jehovah has provided these necessary things: (1) a firm basis for faith in the administration he would provide, (2) a knowledge of the principles of his government, (3) a demonstration of his qualities as Universal Ruler and (4) a sure and unmistakable identification of the Messiah, the One who would be mankind's Deliverer and the King ruling in Jehovah's name. (Galatians 3:24) At the same time a comparison with man-rule has proved the superiority, deservedness and rightness of God's rulership.

ONE NATION SELECTED TO SERVE
FOR THE BENEFIT OF ALL

[13] What means did God use in laying such a foundation? First, he selected one nation, the nation of ancient Israel, to become a living demonstration of his principles and dealings. Thereby Jehovah revealed himself and his marvelous qualities of justice and wisdom when he chastised Israel for their sins, for they proved, for the most part, to be disobedient. (Romans 10:21) Then, too, he exhibited his love, mercy and long-

11, 12. (a) How did God proceed after the Flood? (b) In laying a foundation for his government over the earth, what things has he made it possible for men to see?
13, 14. What did God accomplish for our benefit by using the ancient nation of Israel?

suffering toward them whenever they repented.

[14] Additionally, *Israelite* history demonstrates what happens when God's wise, righteous laws are either obeyed or disobeyed; while *world* history reveals the outcome to those who live without the benefit of the divine law.—1 Corinthians 12:2; Ephesians 4:17-19.

REASON FOR ISRAEL'S SELECTION

[15] Why was Israel, rather than some other nation, selected? Not because they were better, but because of God's love for Abraham their forefather. (Deuteronomy 7:7, 8; 2 Kings 13:23) Some four hundred years after the Flood, Jehovah found Abraham to be a man who accepted God at His word, with unquestioning faith and obedience. (Genesis 15:1, 6; Romans 4:18-22) Consequently, Abraham's offspring through his faithful wife Sarah received the unique blessing of being chosen as the people that Jehovah God would use to accomplish the purpose he had in mind. The promised "seed" would come through Abraham, Isaac and Jacob.

[16] The other nations of that time went their own way of self-rule and disobedience to God. God allowed them to enjoy the sun and rain and the fruitage of the earth. (Acts 14:16, 17; Matthew 5:45) But God did not enter into dealings with them, except when individuals from among them came to him in faith, or when these nations touched upon the affairs of his chosen nation. —Deuteronomy 32:8.

[17] But Jehovah had not forgotten the other

---

15. Did God show partiality in using the nation of Israel? Explain.
16, 17. In dealing with ancient Israel, did God do injustice to the other nations? Explain.

nations. While dealing exclusively with Israel, he was working out a purpose to bless the people of these nations later, although they were completely ignorant of this fact.—Genesis 22:18.

¹⁸ No one can complain about God's selecting one nation to provide this foundation for our faith and understanding today. During this period Israel was blessed above the other nations, it is true. But, by having Jehovah's name placed upon it, that nation also faced a very heavy responsibility that the other nations did not bear. Israel had to account directly to God. The people were severely disciplined by Jehovah when they broke his laws.—Deuteronomy 28:15-68.

¹⁹ Another purpose accomplished by using the one nation was the preserving of the truth. This, God did by keeping Israel separate from the unbelieving peoples around them, by disciplining that nation and holding it together under his Law covenant. He also committed to them his "sacred pronouncements," which we now find in the Bible. (Romans 3:1, 2) In the meantime the other nations, under man-rule, continuously served a wide variety of false gods of their own making, and with a confusing mixture of doctrines. —Psalms 96:5; 115:2-8.

²⁰ Furthermore, all during this time Jehovah was working out matters to provide the finest gift to mankind—the principal "seed" of promise, Christ Jesus, the King of God's kingdom to rule the earth. Through him, God will bring life to all

---

18. In being used and blessed by God, was Israel under heavier judgment?
19. What further benefit was brought to us by God's use of ancient Israel, as shown at Romans 3:1, 2?
20. (a) What primary thing did the law given to Israel accomplish? (Romans 10:4) (b) What other good things do we derive from studying the Hebrew Scriptures?

obedient men. (Acts 17:30, 31) How God's wisdom shines in furnishing an unmistakable identification and therefore a basis for faith in the Messiah when he finally arrived! The Most High provided this positive identification in the genealogy, chronology and prophecy of the Hebrew Scriptures. (John 5:39) Moreover, the historical record preserved in the Hebrew Scriptures not only gives comfort and hope but also serves as a guide for present living. It provides patterns as well as examples for "us upon whom the ends of the systems of things have arrived."—1 Corinthians 10:11; Hebrews 10:1.

JESUS SELECTS ASSOCIATES FOR RULERSHIP

[21] Finally the long-awaited Messiah appeared. As God's anointed one, Jesus Christ was selective, just as God had been, in the people he chose to be his intimate disciples. (Luke 8:38, 39) He was here, it is true, to provide the ransom for the salvation of all men who will accept it. (Matthew 20:28; John 3:16) But he knew that not until later would he be Head of a kingdom that would bring the benefits of his sacrifice to all mankind. And just as any ruler not yet inaugurated into office thinks first of the men he will place in important administrative positions under him, so Jesus was interested, first, in those who would be associated with him in the Kingdom government.—Luke 22:28, 29; John 17:12.

[22] Accordingly, Jesus, through prayer and direction of God's spirit, selected his apostles first. (Luke 6:12-16) These were to be the foundation of an administrative body to operate under his headship.

21, 22. Why was Jesus, when on earth, selective in the choice of his intimate disciples? (Luke 9:57-62)

²³ In reading the Christian Greek Scriptures we observe that the hope held out to all those who accepted the preaching of Jesus and his apostles was that of sharing with Jesus Christ in his Kingdom rule in heaven. (2 Timothy 2:12; Hebrews 3:1; 1 Peter 1:1-4) However, while on earth these disciples would not be *rulers,* but would be known simply as "the congregation of God." They would merely declare God's excellencies to the people.—1 Peter 2:9.

²⁴ So, the long time period following Christ's death and his taking of Kingdom power would be occupied in selecting, training, testing, proving and qualifying those who would reign with Christ. The requirements were very strict. According to the Scriptures, God limited the number of this select administrative body under Jesus Christ to 144,000 persons.—Revelation 14:1-3.

²⁵ Jehovah trains and disciplines these prospective kings and priests through the many tests they undergo. In this way they become fitted exactly for the place he has for them in his government. (Ephesians 2:10; Romans 8:29) Additionally, because of this perfect training and testing he can be sure of their everlasting loyalty and incorruptness in rulership. It is said of them: "No falsehood was found in their mouths; they are without blemish." (Revelation 14:5) This means that their devotion and integrity are free from defect. (Compare Romans 7:25.) They are trustworthy in every respect. Jehovah can safely

23. (a) What hope was held out through the preaching of Jesus and his apostles? (b) Were these disciples to rule over other men while they were on earth? (1 Corinthians 4:8)
24. What primary work of God has been carried on from the time of Christ's resurrection until now?
25. What is the purpose of the severe testing that the prospective members of Christ's Kingdom government have received?

give them immortal heavenly life. (1 Corinthians 15:50-54) But let us now consider how God also had the rest of humankind in mind as he tested and approved those whom he would use as his governmental body.

MERCIFUL RULERS ASSURED

[26] Jesus Christ, the congregation's Head, underwent a most severe test to prove his qualifications. Of him it is said: "We have as high priest, not one who cannot sympathize with our weaknesses, but one who has been tested in all respects like ourselves, but without sin." (Hebrews 4:15) What wisdom and fairness on God's part! The Ruler that he puts over mankind will therefore never deal unjustly or partially.

[27] Also, because of Christ's previous experience in heaven, where he worked with his Father in the creation of all other things, he understands the makeup of men and women. (John 1:10; 2:25) But more than that, by becoming a man of blood and flesh on earth he experienced the service of God under adverse conditions. He fully understands human problems. He knows what it means to suffer. (Hebrews 5:7-9) All men can have full faith in Christ's rulership, knowing that he has undergone the same trials successfully and knows what humans need.—Hebrews 4:16; John 16:33.

[28] Also, consider God's wisdom in his manner of selecting the body of 144,000 associate kings and priests. It has not been a waste of time. During the broad scope of the last nineteen cen-

---

26. How did Christ qualify to become mankind's High Priest and Ruler?
27. What experiences have equipped him to be a ruler in whom we can have full faith?
28. Why has God's allowance of a 1,900-year period until now not been a waste of time?

turies these men and women have been chosen from all walks of life, all races and languages and all backgrounds. There is simply no problem that some of them have not faced and overcome. These, too, will be sympathetic and merciful associate rulers, able to help men and women of all kinds.

FOUNDATION FOR A "NEW EARTH"

[29] Does the mere selection of the last ones of those who will become heavenly kings and priests with Christ complete God's preparations? Does it mean that the thousand-year rule may then begin, and the resurrection of the dead may take place? No, for first God must clean up the earth by destroying the corrupt system of things now existing. However, when he does this, he is not going to leave a "vacuum." That is, he is not going to leave the earth a desolate globe, with no life, no persons serving him, any more than he did so at the Flood. (Isaiah 45:18) Rather, God will have people who survive and who will begin bringing about paradise conditions. They will be on hand when the time comes to welcome back the dead, and they will help them on the way to life.

[30] Who will the survivors of that destruction be? The apostle John, in describing the vision that Christ gave him, says, after speaking of the 144,000 Kingdom heirs: "After these things I saw, and, look! a great crowd, which no man was able to number, out of all nations and tribes and peoples and tongues." The angel bringing the vision then explained who this unnumbered mul-

29. What further preparation must God make in order that his kingdom bring to pass the doing of his will "as in heaven, also upon earth"? (Matthew 6:10)
30. What further group will God gather, to survive the destruction of the present system of things?

titude was: "These are the ones that come out of the great tribulation, and they have washed their robes and made them white in the blood of the Lamb."—Revelation 7:9, 14; Isaiah 2:2-4.

[31] These people will form a nucleus, the "foundation" of a "new earth." (Compare Isaiah 51:16.) Surviving the "great tribulation," they will immediately begin working under the direction of the "new heavens" of Christ and his 144,000 associate kings and priests, to subdue the earth.

31. What part will the "great crowd" play in God's progressive purpose?

Survivors of the great tribulation will be persons who now demonstrate faith in God's promises

They will carry on true worship in the earth as God's representatives, and will introduce the resurrected dead to true worship. They will logically see that there are food and homes ready for these people, and will serve as teachers in the ways of righteousness.

[32] Since the "great crowd" is to survive the "great tribulation," it is obvious that they would be gathered from among people living in the time just prior to the end of this present system of things. This gathering work, then, is also a part of God's preparatory work before the thousand-year reign of Christ begins. Gathering the "great crowd," however, does not take centuries, as did God's dealing with Israel and, later, his gathering of the 144,000 joint heirs with Christ. Nevertheless, it does take time. This selection and gathering are taking place now, and will evidently be completed during the lifetime of one generation. Some of that generation will survive into the period of Christ's thousand-year reign.—Luke 21:32.

[33] Summing up, we see that God has certainly not wasted time. (2 Peter 3:9) He has made it a matter of record that man cannot successfully rule the world. He has demonstrated his patience and his good qualities in the progressive steps he has taken toward bringing in his Kingdom rule. He has shown what kind of government he administers. And he has given us an abundance of

---

32. Who will make up the "great crowd," and when are they selected and gathered?
33, 34. (a) During the time of mankind's history of about 6,000 years, what has God accomplished? (b) Could it be rightly said that "God is dead" or that he is slow?

evidence that Jesus Christ is the principal one of the promised "seed" of Abraham, the Messiah, the King who will rule the earth in righteousness. —Galatians 3:16.

[34] Consequently, those who sincerely want to know Jehovah God can do so. They can gain a firm faith in his purposes, for they have *realities* upon which to base that faith.

Chapter 13

A Pattern of Things to Come

TODAY there is such a maze of laws on the books of most nations that the individual seeking justice is usually unwise to try to be his own lawyer. Besides, "loopholes" exist that usually favor the rich. Would it not be pleasant to live under a law code that was straightforward and simple—in that a court case would not be costly, even for the ordinary man, and where any man, rich or poor, could informally bring his case before the court and get an impartial hearing?

[2] Such was the Mosaic law code that God gave to Israel. Of this law the Bible says: "The judicial decisions of Jehovah are true; they have proved altogether righteous." (Psalm 19:9) The fine quality of Jehovah's judicial decisions can be seen

---

1. What makes it difficult for an individual to get justice under today's legal arrangement?
2, 3. Why is it profitable for us to give consideration to the law that God gave to Israel?

in an examination of a few of the statutes making up this code of a little more than 600 laws.

³ Christians are not under that law given to Israel, but it is profitable to consider it. Why? Because the Law clarifies how Jehovah views matters and it illuminates the principles by which he deals with his creation at all times.

⁴ The administration of the government of Israel was unique in that Jehovah was its supreme and absolute Ruler. He was the King and was, additionally, God, the Head of religion. The prophet Isaiah said: "Jehovah is our Judge, Jehovah is our Statute-giver, Jehovah is our King; he himself will save us."—Isaiah 33:22.

⁵ Idolatry, or the worship of any other god, was therefore at the same time treason, an offense against the government. Likewise, flagrantly violating the law of the land was an act of disrespect toward God, the Head of the nation's worship. A willful violation of the law was tantamount to blasphemy. Thus, *obedience to the law* was a part of *true worship*.

CIVIL RIGHTS

⁶ There were no civil-rights problems under the Law when its judges and rulers obeyed God. It protected the native, the alien resident and even the foreigner staying temporarily in the land. —Exodus 22:21; 23:9; Leviticus 19:33, 34.

⁷ Under the Law the poor man was not deprived of justice because he was poor, nor the rich man simply because he was rich.—Leviticus 19:15; Exodus 23:3.

---

4. What position and authority did Jehovah have in ancient Israel's government?
5. In Israel, how was obedience to the law also a practice of true worship?
6, 7. Describe how civil rights were protected.

KIND CONSIDERATION FOR THE POOR

[8] The economy of Israel was mostly agricultural, each man having his own land inheritance. Some Israelites, through bad management or financial reverses, might become poor and have to sell their land. Some alien residents might also come into bad circumstances.

The Law provided for the poor, requiring that the edges of fields be left for them to glean

In kindness to them, the arrangement was that each farmer, in harvesting, should not reap the edges of his field. He should also leave behind any sheaf of grain forgotten by the harvesters. (Leviticus 19:9, 10; Deuteronomy 24:19-21) This was left as gleanings for the poor person.—Ruth 2:15, 16.

[9] Of course, this took work on the part of the poor person, for gleaning was not easy. Consequently, there were no idle poor on the hands of the government—no dole and no welfare state. (Deuteronomy 15:11; Ruth 2:3, 7) This parallels the Christian principle at 2 Thessalonians 3:10, where we read: "If anyone does not want to work, neither let him eat."

---

8. How did the Law give consideration to the poor?
9, 10. How did all the people benefit from the laws protecting poor persons?

[10] Along with the arrangements for the poor person to earn a living, all citizens were put under obligation to treat needy ones with generosity. This promoted brotherhood and national unity. —Leviticus 25:35-38.

A "SLAVERY" THAT WAS NOT OPPRESSIVE

[11] "Slavery" in Israel was not like the oppressive slavery known in more recent times. It was actually a way of protecting the family who, through financial reverses or calamity, were obliged to sell their land inheritance and who eventually used up the money received from the sale and were destitute. Or, they might get heavily into debt. Then, instead of being self-employed as they had been, the family, or certain members thereof, could go into "slavery." But this slavery was very much like our modern-day principle of employment, working for another person, which for many is a form of 'economic slavery.'

[12] For example, the Hebrew "slave" had to be treated, not like property, but as a "hired laborer." Furthermore, he was to be released after six years' servitude. (Leviticus 25:39-43) At his release his master or "employer" had to give him material things, as he was able, to help the man and his family to make a fresh start. (Deuteronomy 15:12-15) By this arrangement a family could avoid being destitute and could have food and clothing until such time as they could stand on their own.

[13] Moreover, the person, while in "slavery,"

11. In ancient Israel, why was slavery not harsh and oppressive, as it has been in more recent times?
12. What was the arrangement for Hebrew "slaves"?
13. (a) What was the possibility of freedom before the normal six years of servitude was fulfilled? (b) What protection was provided for young Hebrew girls who were slaves?

could engage in projects or other business or investments, so that in some cases a man was able to buy himself out of servitude. Or a near relative could pay off any indebtedness he might have, thereby releasing the man as a free person. (Leviticus 25:47-54) A daughter who went into "slavery" often was taken as the wife of her master. She had to be given full dues as was the case with any wife.—Exodus 21:7-11.

PROTECTION FOR WOMEN

[14] Women were protected by the marriage laws. A man had to have valid cause to divorce his wife, and additionally was required to give her a certificate of divorce. The certificate of divorce protected her from any false charges in case of remarriage.—Deuteronomy 24:1; see Jesus' explanation about divorce at Matthew 19:3-9.

[15] A man who seduced a virgin girl, not engaged to marry, had to marry her, at her father's discretion, and could never divorce her. (Deuteronomy 22:28, 29; Exodus 22:16, 17) In the case of an engaged woman, a death penalty for the man protected her from sexual assault, which was considered as serious as murder.—Deuteronomy 22:25-27.

[16] Although polygamy was allowed, it was regulated for the woman's benefit. Polygamy, a practice of long standing, was tolerated because it was not God's time to straighten out all things. God waited until the time of Christianity to restore the original state of monogamy. (1 Co-

14. How was a divorced woman protected?
15. What laws served as a deterrent to fornication?
16. (a) Was polygamy the original arrangement of God? (Matthew 19:4-6) (b) Why did God tolerate polygamy in ancient Israel?

rinthians 7:2) God's way has been to teach and lead his people as they were able to understand and accept correction of their ways. Jesus said to his disciples, at John 16:12: "I have many things yet to say to you, but you are not able to bear them at present." Thus, after Jesus' death and resurrection, many things were clarified and made straight for them.

[17] In a polygamous marriage, one of the wives was often favored by the husband. But protection was given by the Law to the less loved wife. For example, if her son was the father's firstborn he would not be deprived of his firstborn rights, for the father could not give them to a son later born to a favorite wife.—Deuteronomy 21:15-17.

[18] Even women in enemy cities were not sexually molested. Nor were prostitutes found in the vicinity of army camps, for sex relations were forbidden to soldiers engaged in war operations. —Deuteronomy 21:10-14.

CRIMINAL LAWS

[19] The criminal laws were far finer than those on statute books today. There were no prisons provided for under the Law. Only later, during the rule of the kings, were prisons instituted, improperly, in Israel. (Jeremiah 37:15, 16; 38:6, 28) Since no prison sentence was given for any crime, it meant that no criminals were being fed and housed at the expense of the hardworking people who obeyed the law.

---

17. How was the less loved wife in a polygamous marriage protected?
18. How were women, even among Israel's enemies, protected?
19. What was the advantage of there being no prisons in ancient Israel?

[20] If a man stole from his fellowman, he was not imprisoned. In this way he was able to work and pay for what he stole. His victim suffered no loss. In addition, the thief was required to pay double or more for what he stole, depending upon the item stolen and his disposition of it. (Exodus 22:1, 4, 7) If he did not pay, he was sold into slavery. He had to work for his victim or for another Israelite until he had paid off the judgment against him for what he had stolen. (Exodus 22:3) If he presumptuously refused to follow through on his sentence, he would be put to death. (Deuteronomy 17:12) This law not only helped the victim of the thief but also was a strong deterrent to stealing.

[21] Life was considered sacred under the Law. A deliberate murderer could in no way be exonerated. He was to be put to death without fail. Thus in Numbers 35:30-33 we read: "Every fatal striker of a soul should be slain as a murderer at the mouth of witnesses, and one witness may not testify against a soul for him to die. And you must take no ransom for the soul of a murderer who is deserving to die, for without fail he should be put to death. . . . And you must not pollute the land in which you are; because it is blood that pollutes the land, and for the land there may be no atonement respecting the blood that has been spilled upon it except by the blood of the one spilling it." This law removed such a wicked person from Israelite society. He did not run free to commit more murders. The accidental

---

20. What was the penalty for stealing, and what benefits did it bring?
21. (a) What was the penalty for deliberate murder? (b) What was the arrangement for the accidental manslayer?

manslayer, however, could receive mercy.—Numbers 35:9-15, 22-29.

²² Even the unsolved murder was not allowed to go unatoned for. The city nearest the scene of the slaying was considered as bloodguilty and under a curse unless the city elders performed the ceremony required, to receive removal of community bloodguilt before God. Thus the sacredness of life was deeply impressed upon the people. —Deuteronomy 21:1-9.

²³ One's person was considered inviolable. Kidnapping was a capital crime. The kidnapper in whose hand the person was found or who had sold the kidnapped one into slavery was to be put to death without fail.—Exodus 21:16; Deuteronomy 24:7.

NO DELINQUENCY

²⁴ When the nation followed the Law, there were few problems of juvenile delinquency. The essential unit of the nation was the family. Great respect for the parents, as well as for the chieftains of the nation, was taught. (Exodus 20:12; 22:28) Mob action was condemned. (Exodus 23:1, 2) A son of responsible age who was incurably rebellious, perhaps becoming a glutton and a drunkard, was to be executed. (Deuteronomy 21:18-21) Whoever struck his father or mother, or called down evil upon them, was to be put to death. (Exodus 21:15, 17; Leviticus 20:9) Respect for the home and family resulted in respect for the nation's rulers, particularly its Chief Ruler, Jehovah God.

22. How was the sacredness of life especially emphasized?
23. Describe the law governing kidnapping.
24. How was respect for the family maintained, and with what result?

RESPECT FOR PROPERTY RIGHTS

25 In modern times, the practice popularly followed in regard to lost items is 'finders keepers.' But in Israel, anyone who found an animal or some item was required to restore it to its owner. If the owner lived far away and was unknown, then the item was to be kept until the owner searched for it. (Deuteronomy 22:1-3) In order to aid the owner who came to the village looking for his lost property, the finder would, of course, have to report to the city elders or officials that he had it.

26 The sanctity of the home was most highly respected. A man could not collect a debt by going into the debtor's house to get what had been pledged as security. The creditor had to wait outside and let the man bring out the pledged article to him. (Deuteronomy 24:10, 11) Neither could a creditor foreclose on one's immediate means of living or one's essential clothing, since a poor man might have only some grain to grind to feed his family, or only one outer garment as a covering.

27 On this point it is written in Deuteronomy 24:6, 12, 13: "No one should seize a hand mill or its upper grindstone as a pledge, because it is a soul that he is seizing as a pledge. And if the man is in trouble, you must not go to bed with his pledge. You should by all means return the pledge to him as soon as the sun sets, and he must go to bed in his garment, and he must bless you; and it will mean righteousness for you before Jehovah your God."

---

25. How were lost-and-found items handled?
26, 27. (a) What respect was maintained for a man's home and property? (b) Of what benefit were these laws to the poor?

KINDNESS TO ANIMALS

[28] Animals were also given kind consideration. If a man saw a domestic animal in distress he was required to help it, even if it belonged to an enemy of his. (Exodus 23:4, 5; Deuteronomy 22:4) Beasts of burden were not to be overworked or mistreated. (Deuteronomy 22:10; Proverbs 12:10) The bull was not to be muzzled so that he could not enjoy the fruits of his labor when threshing grain. (Deuteronomy 25:4) Kindness to wild animals was also fostered. A man was not to remove both a mother bird and her eggs, thereby wiping out the family. (Deuteronomy 22:6, 7) Among domestic animals an individual was not to slaughter a bull or a sheep and its young on the same day. All of this was a deterrent to a spirit of cruelty.—Leviticus 22:28; compare God's consideration for animals as expressed at Jonah 4:11 and Leviticus 25:4, 5, 7.

ZEAL FOR TRUTH

[29] In the interests of justice and mercy, a witness in a legal case was required to testify to whatever he knew about the case. If he did not do so he would be subject to a curse publicly uttered by the judges. Such a curse, God would enforce. (Leviticus 5:1; Proverbs 29:24) He was not to commit perjury, for this was lying "before Jehovah." If accusations made against another were found to be deliberately false, the accuser would suffer the same penalty that would have been meted out to the one falsely accused.

[30] Accordingly, we read in Deuteronomy 19:16-19: "In case a witness scheming violence should

28. How did God show his thoughtfulness and kindness in his laws regarding animals?
29, 30. What laws governed witnesses in legal cases?

rise up against a man to bring a charge of revolt against him, the two men who have the dispute must also stand *before Jehovah,* before the priests and the judges who will be acting in those days. And the judges must search thoroughly, and if the witness is a false witness and has brought a false charge against his brother, *you must also do to him just as he had schemed to do to his brother,* and you must clear away what is bad from your midst."

[31] No one could be put to death on circumstantial evidence alone. There had to be at least two eyewitnesses to establish the truth. (Deuteronomy 17:6; 19:15) The witnesses against a man found guilty of a capital crime were to be the first to share in stoning the man to death. This law promoted zeal for righteousness in Israel. Not only the judges, but every citizen was thus required to demonstrate his desire to keep the land clean from bloodguilt before God. It was also a deterrent to false, hasty or careless testimony. Good was derived from the law in Deuteronomy 17:7, which reads: "The hand of the witnesses first of all should come upon him to put him to death, and the hand of all the people afterward; and you must clear out what is bad from your midst."

FORBIDDEN SEXUAL RELATIONS

[32] Adultery was punishable by death for both parties. (Leviticus 20:10) The revolting practices of homosexuality and bestiality incurred the death penalty, according to Leviticus 20:13, 15, where it is written: "When a man lies down with

---

31. What other laws promoted zeal for righteousness and also tended to prevent false or careless testimony in a legal case?
32. What illicit sexual relations were punishable by death?

a male the same as one lies down with a woman, both of them have done a detestable thing. They should be put to death without fail. Their own blood is upon them. And where a man gives his seminal emission to a beast, he should be put to death without fail, and you should kill the beast." —See also Leviticus 20:16, 17; Romans 1:24-28.

CLEANNESS

[33] The Law enjoined upon the people not only moral cleanness but also physical cleanliness. The laws on cleanness required the Israelites to destroy earthenware vessels that came into contact with any animal that died of itself. Other vessels as well as garments had to be washed. Such a law kept the Israelites ever alert to be clean. Persons with communicable diseases were quarantined. (Leviticus 13:4, 5, 21, 26) Infected garments and houses were quarantined, and in some cases, destroyed. (Leviticus 13:47-52, 55; 14:38, 45) No blood was to be eaten.—Leviticus 7:26.

[34] From a medical viewpoint, the law of sanitation and quarantine, along with the moral laws and the prohibition on blood, were marvelous protections from typhoid, typhus, bubonic plague, hepatitis, gonorrhea and syphilis and a host of other diseases.

MERCY TO REPENTANT ONES

[35] The Law was not harsh or inflexible. Judges were given latitude to show mercy. If a man sinned against his fellowman, and then repented, he could be restored to God's favor by first

33, 34. How did the Law promote physical cleanliness?
35. Were the judges in legal cases allowed latitude to show mercy, depending on the circumstances?

straightening out matters with the injured party and then by presenting a guilt offering to Jehovah. (Leviticus 6:2-7) Jesus Christ alluded to this law when he said: "If, then, you are bringing your gift to the altar and you there remember that your brother has something against you, leave your gift there in front of the altar, and go away; first make your peace with your brother, and then, when you have come back, offer up your gift." (Matthew 5:23, 24) Today, servants of God cannot have peace with Him if they are doing wrong toward their fellowman.

JUBILEE YEAR

[36] The Jubilee, which occurred every fiftieth year, was a time of rejoicing. All land inheritances that had been "sold" were returned to their owners. Hebrew slaves were released, even if their six years' servitude was not yet fulfilled. (Leviticus 25:8-13, 39-41) This law had the grand

Announcement of the Jubilee year required that all lands be returned to their original owners

36. What fine things did the Jubilee year law provide?

effect of restoring the economy to the original, balanced state that God established when Israel entered the Promised Land. It prevented the situation we see in many lands today—an extremely rich landowner class and an extremely poor "serf" class. No land monopoly was possible when the law was enforced.

[37] Thus the Law made a citizen a free man. Every family was safe from falling into a state of perpetual poverty. The family dignity was maintained, the family spirituality was kept high. The father could spend time with the family, the sabbath days and sabbath years providing time for attention to such things as teaching the children. So, while Christians are not under the Mosaic law today, it provides a glimpse of God's ways and dealings and a "shadow of the good things to come."—Hebrews 10:1.

---

37. In summary, what reason could be given that we should study God's law to Israel?

Chapter 14

The Elimination of Crime and Injustice

IS IT not true that, however good you try to be, you are surrounded by conditions that make it hard for you? In the business world, with its fight for economic survival, there is pressure to cheat in order to meet competition. In everyday

---

1. How does this world make it difficult to live according to what is right?

life we observe immorality, drug abuse, bad language, hatred and the spirit of revenge. And these practices, to a large degree, are made to seem normal and right by the entertainment world and the propaganda channels.

² Nevertheless, many people realize the strong effect that bad environment has and often they move from one neighborhood to another hoping to find better conditions, particularly for the benefit of their children. They know that a bad environment can put a strain on the good principles that they have taught their children.

³ Even with ancient Israel under the Mosaic law, as good as it was, the environment was not always favorable to faithful worship of God. Israel was surrounded by idol-worshiping nations. (Deuteronomy 13:6, 7, 12, 13) The Israelites were sinners, as were all mankind. And while the Law helped to keep many of them firm in the true worship of God, the majority proved disobedient. (2 Chronicles 36:15, 16) They gave in to their environment. Furthermore, Satan the Devil has been a strong influence during the centuries since the first man's downfall, hindering the people from getting a knowledge of God. The apostle Paul wrote:

⁴ "If, now, the good news we declare is in fact veiled, it is veiled among those who are perishing, among whom the god of this system of things has blinded the minds of the unbelievers, that the illumination of the glorious good news about the Christ, who is the image of God, might not shine through."—2 Corinthians 4:3, 4.

2. Do people recognize the effect that a bad environment has?
3, 4. (a) How did ancient Israel's environment affect them? (b) What has been the chief factor in producing bad environment?

A CHANGED ENVIRONMENT

⁵ So it is evident that a changed environment would do much to help sinful humans to 'make their minds over' to obey the good principles of God. (Romans 12:2) God purposes to bring about just such an environment under the thousand-year reign of Jesus Christ.

⁶ First, the wicked system of things must pass away, being destroyed by God. (1 John 2:17) Then the Devil, "the god of this system of things," must be bound so that he cannot influence mankind to rebel against Jehovah God. (Revelation 20:1, 2) He has done this by deceiving them and by playing on their imperfections to cause them to sin, which brings death.—Revelation 12:9; Hebrews 2:14, 15.

⁷ The Psalms give us prophetic glimpses of the conditions that will prevail when Christ rules earth as King:

⁸ "In his days the righteous one will sprout, and the abundance of peace." "There will come to be plenty of grain on the earth." "Trueness itself will sprout out of the very earth, and righteousness itself will look down from the very heavens. Also, Jehovah, for his part, will give what is good, and our own land will give its yield."—Psalms 72:7, 16; 85:11, 12.

⁹ And the prophet Isaiah wrote of Jesus Christ:

¹⁰ "The princely rule will come to be upon his shoulder. And his name will be called Wonderful Counselor, Mighty God, Eternal Father, Prince of Peace. To the abundance of the princely rule and

5, 6. What does God purpose to do about our present environment?
7-12. Describe the conditions to be brought about by Christ's Kingdom rule.

to peace there will be no end, upon the throne of David and upon his kingdom in order to establish it firmly and to sustain it by means of justice and by means of righteousness, from now on and to time indefinite. The very zeal of Jehovah of armies will do this."—Isaiah 9:6, 7.

[11] Illustrating the helpful environment that the new system of things will bring, Isaiah says:

[12] "The path of the righteous one is uprightness. You being upright, *you will smooth out the very course* of a righteous one. Yes, for the path of your judgments, O Jehovah, we have hoped in you . . . When there are judgments from you for the earth, righteousness is what the inhabitants of the productive land will certainly learn."—Isaiah 26:7-9.

Bad environment contributes to crime

¹³ With Jehovah's judgments being declared and enforced in all the earth, the "great crowd" who survive the destruction of the present system of things into that new system

13. Will it be easier for the resurrected people to learn the truth about God than it was in their previous life? Why?

Under the rulership of Jesus Christ, wholesome environment will encourage good conduct

will be able to teach the resurrected ones without hindrance from wicked opposers of God and of Christ. (Revelation 7:9, 10, 14-16) With justice and peace prevailing, how much clearer the truth will stand out. How much more readily those listeners can obey and "smooth out" their course of life!

[14] In our present time, men commit acts of criminality, and some become what we call 'hardened criminals.' All persons have weaknesses toward sin, in one direction or another. (Romans 6:19) All received these weaknesses through genetic inheritance. (Psalm 51:5) A person may have a tendency, for example, toward an uncontrolled temper and violence. Some are more aggressive than others, inclining to 'take the law into their own hands' when they feel that an injustice has been done. Others are more easily ensnared by immorality, overuse of alcohol, and so forth. But relatively few of these persons would ordinarily do criminal acts. It takes bad environment as a 'culture medium' in which bad tendencies are fed and encouraged, along with a circumstance that will "trigger" or give opportunity or incentive for the lawless action.—1 Corinthians 15:33.

[15] But when this wicked world is eliminated and Satan is bound so that he cannot interfere, mankind can then be gradually rehabilitated. People's good tendencies will be fed and encouraged by the good environment; the bad traits will be discouraged. Bad desires and acts will be 'out of

14. How has this system of things accentuated the bad tendencies we have inherited from imperfect parents?
15. (a) How will the environment under Christ's kingdom build up good traits? (b) What will have to be done by the individual in order for him to be rehabilitated?

place' and viewed as something to be put aside. However, it will require effort on a person's part to 'put away anger, badness and abusive speech' and to 'clothe himself with the new personality, which through accurate knowledge is being made new according to the image of the One who created it.' (Colossians 3:8-10) One must have a strong desire to change, for God wants willingly obedient subjects. (Psalm 81:11-13) Under the administration of Christ and his associate kings and priests the person making the changes will be helped in every way possible, not hindered in his efforts.—Revelation 7:17.

THOSE WHO WILL FAIL TO GET LIFE

[16] Only persons who commit 'blasphemy against the holy spirit' will die in that new system of things. (Matthew 12:31, 32) This sin is a deliberate, willful, rebellious, blasphemous action against God. How, then, is it 'against the holy spirit'?

[17] To illustrate, consider the Pharisees. They brought themselves into great danger of committing this sin, and some of them evidently did. They might have disbelieved in Jesus' Messiahship simply through lack of faith, as was the case with Saul, who later became the apostle Paul. (1 Timothy 1:12, 13) But when Jesus spoke about unforgivable sin, the Pharisees had just witnessed the powerful words and works of Jesus as the result of God's spirit upon him. When they *saw* and *knew* that God's spirit was working through Jesus, they were actually guilty of blasphemy

16, 17. (a) Who will fail to get everlasting life in the new system of things? (b) When Jesus was on earth, how were the religious leaders putting themselves in great danger?

against the holy spirit. How? They deliberately attributed Jesus' works to the power of the demons. The Pharisees had a wholly selfish purpose in mind. They wanted to mislead the people so they could hold their position of dominance. —Matthew 12:22-30.

[18] This could be the case with some who become Christians and then deliberately turn from God's pure worship. Hebrews 10:26, 27 states that "if we practice sin willfully after having received the accurate knowledge of the truth, there is no longer any sacrifice for sins left, but there is a certain fearful expectation of judgment."—Compare Hebrews 6:4-6.

[19] The apostle John also refers to a "sin that does incur death" as contrasted with one that does not. (1 John 5:16, 17; compare Numbers 15:30.) A true Christian will have no association with a person professing to be a Christian who, from the evidence he sees, seems to be blaspheming God's spirit, apparently sinning *deliberately and without signs of repentance*. (2 John 9-11) The Christian will not pray in such a person's behalf. However, he cannot read an individual's heart, and cannot judge that a person has actually committed the unforgivable sin. He cannot know for sure that the individual will not repent later on. He recognizes that Christ acts as Judge for God, and he can search the "kidneys" (the innermost emotions and thoughts), and the "heart" (the primary seat of motivation), and Christ can determine whether one has committed

18. Could a Christian lose out on eternal life?
19. (a) What is a 'sin that incurs death'? (b) How should a true Christian view a person who is apparently committing that kind of sin? (c) Can a Christian judge that a person has committed the unforgivable sin? Explain.

blasphemy against the holy spirit.—Revelation 2:23; John 5:22, 30.

[20] Such incorrigible, irreformable persons will be put to death during Christ's thousand-year reign. Their execution as being permanent is represented in the Scriptures by their being hurled into the symbolic "lake of fire," which is the "second death," as distinguished from the death inherited from Adam. (Revelation 20:14, 15) Consequently, disturbers of the peace of that new system of things will not be allowed to remain to cause trouble.

A BETTER LIFE EVEN NOW

[21] But, to those now reading this book we say, as the apostle said to some who were seeking to become mature servants of God: "However, in your case, beloved ones, we are convinced of better things and things accompanied with salvation." (Hebrews 6:9) We do not have to wait until Christ's thousand-year reign to get a good start in serving God. We can and should do that now.

[22] The apostle further said: "Godly devotion is beneficial for all things, as *it holds promise of the life now* and that which is to come." (1 Timothy 4:8) We can be free from many entanglements of the world; we can have peace of mind and a purpose in life. We can enjoy life, along with better relations with our family and our fellowmen. But more than that, we can look with anticipation to possible survival through the coming "great tribulation" without dying and with cer-

---

20. How will irreformable, unrepentant sinners be dealt with during Christ's thousand-year reign?
21, 22. (a) Does one need to wait until Christ's thousand-year reign to live a better, happier life? (b) Discuss the apostle Paul's words on this matter at 1 Timothy 4:8.

tainty of life in full measure in God's new system of things.

[23] We are in a position similar to that of the nation of Israel when about to enter the Promised Land. Moses told them: "This commandment that I am commanding you today is not too difficult for you, nor is it far away. It is not in the heavens, so as to result in saying, 'Who will ascend for us into the heavens and get it for us, that he may let us hear it that we may do it?' Neither is it on the other side of the sea, so as to result in saying, 'Who will pass over for us to the other side of the sea and get it for us, that he may let us hear it that we may do it?' For the word is very near you, in your own mouth and in your own heart, that you may do it."—Deuteronomy 30:11-14.

[24] It is not really difficult for you to know what God requires of you and to do it. Jesus Christ will help you if you exercise faith and act on this faith. (Matthew 11:28-30) You do not have to have someone go to heaven to get the message needed. Jesus Christ has done so and we have his commandments in the Bible. You do not have to travel to some distant land—"on the other side of the sea"—to get wisdom or philosophy from men there. You do not have to get a higher education, nor search into every religion, present and past, to find the truth. You have read about God's purpose in the Bible. It is in your own mouth and heart. It is "this good news of the kingdom." (Matthew 24:14) As Christ's apostle said: "If you publicly declare that 'word in your

---

23, 24. (a) Having seen what God's Word says, should we wait or search somewhere else for the truth? (b) Do we need to look for another Messiah, or for some great man to stand up for our deliverance? (c) What, then, is the right thing to do?

own mouth,' that Jesus is Lord, and exercise faith in your heart that God raised him up from the dead, you will be saved. For with the heart one exercises faith for righteousness, but with the mouth one makes public declaration for salvation." —Romans 10:5-10.

²⁵ So God requires no great and mighty acts from you, but he says: "He has told you, O earthling man, what is good. And what is Jehovah asking back from you but to exercise justice and to love kindness and to be modest in walking with your God?" (Micah 6:8) Is this not reasonable—really what everyone *ought* to do?

²⁶ Therefore, you can get a head start now, eliminating injustice from your own life. To avoid being swerved from your course by bad environment, you will need to get away from close association with those who carry on bad things. Paul wrote to persons who were trying to serve God: "In my letter I wrote you to quit mixing in company with fornicators, not meaning entirely with the fornicators of this world or the greedy persons and extortioners or idolaters. Otherwise, you would actually have to get out of the world." (1 Corinthians 5:9, 10) You may have friends and work associates who do wrong things, and of course you cannot completely get away from association with them. But you would not associate with them in wrongdoing, or constantly mix intimately in company with them. The company to seek is the good association of

25. Is God requiring something great from us, or what does he require?
26, 27. What are some things we can do to get a head start now?

Christians, whom you observe doing right things. This will strengthen you.—Hebrews 13:7.

²⁷ Having done these things, then stay firmly in this course. Trust in God and wait upon him to wipe out injustice, crime and unhappiness completely in his righteous new system of things. —Isaiah 32:1, 16-18.

Chapter 15

The End of Sickness and Death

OF ALL the things that have brought sorrow and suffering to humankind, sickness and death take the lead. Even the *fear* of death has kept people in a form of bondage, and threats of death have forced many to commit acts in violation of their consciences—for example, under Nazi rule, when some people were terrorized into betraying their own friends. (Hebrews 2:15) What relief humankind will experience when these enemies, sickness and death, are abolished! —1 Corinthians 15:26.

² Only the Creator can help people out of this sad situation. And not only has he promised to do so, but he has laid the foundation for complete, permanent removal of death under the rule of

1. What has fear of death often caused people to do?
2, 3. (a) Doing away with death will eliminate what other undesirable things? (b) From what does God's promise to abolish death liberate us now?

the "new heavens" of Jesus Christ and his associate kings and priests. God promises humankind that "he will wipe out every tear from their eyes, and death will be no more, neither will mourning nor outcry nor pain be anymore." He adds, to give us faith and assurance: "These words are faithful and true." (Revelation 21:4, 5) With the removal of sickness and death, the debilitating effects of old age, with its wrinkled skin and gray hair, will also disappear.

³ If we know and believe this divine promise, it removes much of the sadness that death brings. We will not "sorrow just as the rest also do who have no hope."—1 Thessalonians 4:13.

NOT A NEW HOPE

⁴ This hope is not new. Men and women who served God thousands of years ago had this hope that comforted and strengthened them. While they knew that they would die, they also had faith in God that they would be brought back with opportunity for everlasting life. Some of these faithful people were actually eyewitnesses to resurrections that God performed through his prophets and through Jesus and the apostles. Of course, those resurrected ones eventually died again. But God's servants then were awaiting a "better resurrection" under the Messianic kingdom, when it will not be necessary to die again, except for willful disobedience.—Hebrews 11:16, 35.

⁵ Abraham demonstrated faith in the resur-

4. Why can we say that the hope that death will be abolished is not a new hope?
5. What evidence do we have that Abraham, Job and Daniel had assurance that, when they died, they would not remain dead forever?

**When Jesus Christ was on earth, he actually
brought dead persons back to life**

rection in an outstanding way. (Hebrews 11:17-
19) Faithful, enduring Job spoke of being in
Sheol, the grave, and of being remembered by
God at His set time. (Job 14:13) And when the
prophet Daniel asked for understanding of his
long-range prophecy, which was to be fulfilled at
"the time of the end," God's angel told him: "You
will rest, but *you will stand up for your lot at the
end of the days*."—Daniel 12:8, 9, 13.

WHO WILL RECEIVE AN EARTHLY RESURRECTION?

[6] Resurrection from death will be only the first step in God's purpose to rehabilitate those who have died. They will come forth from the grave to be welcomed and received by the "great crowd" of survivors of the "great tribulation," after the destruction of the present wicked system of things. There will be two groups of persons resurrected to live again on earth: (1) People who have proved faithful to God in the past, among whom are those mentioned in the eleventh chapter of Hebrews, and (2) those who had, before death, never been servants of God. "There is going to be a resurrection of both the righteous and the unrighteous," said the apostle Paul. (Acts 24:15) The first group will have no trouble learning and taking hold of God's provisions for life through Christ's sacrifice. They will gladly render obedience to the laws in existence then. Such faithful ones are even now, while still in the grave, counted as "living" by God, because he is sure to resurrect them.—Luke 20:37, 38.

[7] Persons who had not previously served God will, after being resurrected, have to learn about Jehovah the true God and his kind provisions through Jesus Christ. The "great crowd" of tribulation survivors will be responsible to teach them. (Romans 10:14) The good news will have to be made clear to these resurrected ones, for God has declared that "in the name of Jesus every knee should bend of those in heaven and those on earth and those *under the ground* [in the grave],

---

6. (a) What two general groups of people will receive an earthly resurrection? (b) At their resurrection, what will be the attitude of those who had, before death, been servants of God? 7. What will be done for the resurrected ones who had not served God in the past?

and every tongue should openly acknowledge that Jesus Christ is Lord to the glory of God the Father."—Philippians 2:10, 11.

[8] The resurrected ones will be required to be obedient to the laws then in force and will be judged "out of those things written in the scrolls according to their deeds." (Revelation 20:12) The "scrolls" apparently represent God's revelation of his will for humankind during that thousand-year period.

PERFECTION NOT IMMEDIATELY REACHED

[9] The members of the "great crowd" will not be perfected immediately after the "great tribulation" is over. But they survive the destruction of this system of things because of their faith and obedience, and form the "foundation" of the "new earth." (Revelation 7:14-17; compare Isaiah 51:16.) So they will undoubtedly go right ahead in a faithful way and will make rapid strides toward perfection as they follow the things written in the "scrolls."—Psalm 37:30, 31.

[10] What about the members of this "great crowd" who have serious disabilities, such as heart disease, paralysis, blindness, loss of arms or legs, and so forth? It is reasonable to believe that they will receive early healing of these defects. When on earth, Jesus illustrated such healing. He *instantly* healed withered hands and arms, strengthened paralyzed limbs and restored sight to blind eyes. These body parts did not gradually grow back. (Luke 6:8-10; John 5:5-9) Likewise,

---

8. Will the resurrected ones be judged on the basis of their past deeds, or on what basis?
9. What will be the situation of the "great crowd"?
10. What will be done about major disabilities that the members of the "great crowd" as well as the resurrected ones have had?

the resurrected ones will logically come back with sound bodies. This was also true of all those whom the Scriptures report as being resurrected. (Luke 8:54, 55) Lazarus, for example, was partially decayed, but he came back from the grave with decayed parts renewed. (John 11:39-44) God made the following promise to his people whom he purposed to restore to their land in ancient times: "No resident will say: 'I am sick.' The people that are dwelling in the land will be those pardoned for their error." People will be able to do the normal things of life even though not perfect as yet.—Isaiah 33:24.

HOW PERFECTION COMES ABOUT

[11] However, full perfection of body will evidently come only as the individual, because of his faith in Christ, makes spiritual progress in 'putting on the new personality.' Even though a person has been healed of major disabilities, as he practices that which is right he will come nearer and nearer to perfection. He will be regularly partaking of God's provision for his healing by means of Christ's atonement sacrifice. (Revelation 22:2) Christ will mercifully remove all that one's imperfections. This spiritual change will have to be made first, because sin is the cause of death, and a person cannot be perfect in physical body until sin is completely removed from his personality. The Bible always links sickness with sin.—Luke 5:18-25; 1 Corinthians 15:56; Romans 6:23.

[12] The apostle Paul describes the "fight" carried

---

11. (a) How will perfection be attained? (b) Why does a spiritual change have to be made before physical healing takes place?
12. What fight does each servant of God now have in making over his personality, and why?

on now by each one who tries to make over his personality, to become fully pleasing to God. He says: "What I wish, this I do not practice; but what I hate is what I do. . . . The good that I wish I do not do, but the bad that I do not wish is what I practice. . . . The one working it out is no longer I, but the sin dwelling in me." (Romans 7:15-20) Through inheritance, all humans have been brought forth "with error," in sin. (Psalm 51:5) Also, all have added to that sin during their own course of life, the environment wrongly influencing them.

[13] Even today a person can genuinely get rid of the things that he has 'picked up' from his environment, with the help of God's Word, His spirit and his own association with God's servants. But it is different with the things that come through his genetic makeup, that are a part of him, physically and mentally. True, he can fight these faults with considerable success, for the apostles tell us that we can 'make our minds over,' "put on the new personality," 'produce the fruits of the spirit,' "hold a good conscience" and 'maintain fine conduct.' (Romans 12:2; Ephesians 4:24; Galatians 5:22, 23; 1 Peter 3:16; 2:12) But we cannot *completely* wipe out these bad inherited tendencies merely through such effort. The apostle said of his situation: "Miserable man that I am! Who will rescue me from the body undergoing this death? Thanks to God through Jesus Christ our Lord! So, then, with my mind I myself am a slave to God's law, but with my flesh to sin's law."—Romans 7:24, 25.

---

13. What can a person do about (a) the bad tendencies he has 'picked up' from his environment? (b) his inherited tendencies that are bad?

¹⁴ In this present time, the Christian can receive forgiveness for his sins through faith in Jesus Christ and the sacrifice of his life for our errors. And he must follow up his prayers requesting forgiveness by doing his best to align himself with the right course. He can never let up in the fight against wrong inclinations, and with the help of God's spirit it need not be a losing battle. His conscience can be clean. (Romans 8:2, 11-13; Hebrews 9:14) But in the new system of things Christ will administer the *full benefit* of His sacrifice so that the inherited weaknesses, the genetic "misinformation" received from a person's ancestors, will be corrected. He will be healed in every respect. What a relief! What a deliverance when a person will be able to do exactly the good it is in his heart to do, all the time! Thanks, indeed, to God through Jesus Christ.

¹⁵ So, during the thousand-year reign of Christ, an individual can gradually become less and less burdened with sinful tendencies. He will more and more do the right thing. Then, when perfection is reached, it will no longer be a *fight* to do the right thing. It will be natural to do right. A person will not be in the least inclined to steal, to commit immorality, to hate or slander others. The apostle Paul said about the Mosaic law, which legislated against these things: "Now we know that the Law is fine provided one handles it lawfully in the knowledge of this fact, that law

14. (a) When a Christian's inherited weaknesses cause him to sin, what can he do to remain in God's favor? (b) How will one be finally delivered from all inherited weaknesses, which cause sin and distress?
15. (a) When will it no longer be a *fight* for a person to do the right thing at all times? (b) How does the apostle Paul highlight this point at 1 Timothy 1:8, 9? (c) How was Jesus an example of the fact that a righteous man does not need a code of laws forbidding murder, theft, and so forth?

is promulgated, not for a righteous man, but for persons lawless and unruly, ungodly and sinners." (1 Timothy 1:8, 9) A perfect person needs no law to warn him not to do these wicked things. When Jesus was on earth, it was the natural thing for him to do what is right. He 'loved righteousness and hated lawlessness.' (Hebrews 1:9) He had an immediate, heart-motivated reaction to do good and to reject bad. Consider the account of his temptation by Satan and also Peter's mistaken effort to get Jesus to avoid that which God had set before Jesus to do.—Matthew 4:1-11; 16:21-23.

RECEIVING RESURRECTED ONES

[16] As to the resurrected ones, God will accurately "re-create" each individual with his entire life pattern, personality and memory just as it was. The one resurrected will be able to identify himself as the same person. Also, his former associates will know him by his appearance and characteristics. He can then resume life after the interruption caused by his death, possessing the same motivations, leanings and traits that he displayed beforehand. However, his past sins and mistakes will not be brought up as charges against him. Why not? Because God's purpose in bringing him back to earth is to provide opportunity for him to take advantage of Christ's sacrifice and be freed of sin. Yet, what the individual did in the past, if bad, would have its effect on his personality, and the resulting bad traits would have to be overcome. The more unrighteous his past course was, the more he will have to change. Some

---

16. (a) Will resurrected persons be identifiable to themselves and their friends? (b) What is God's purpose in bringing a person back to earth by a resurrection? (c) Though a resurrected person will not be judged by his past deeds, will such past performance have any effect on his life after resurrection?

may not take advantage of the opportunity to change.—Isaiah 26:10.

¹⁷ To the person who is resurrected, the time period that he was dead would be, to him, only an instant, since death is a nonexistence. It is likened in the Bible to a deep sleep. (John 11: 11-14; 1 Thessalonians 4:13, 14; Ecclesiastes 9:5, 10) Thousands of years, or a day, would seem like only a moment of time. To the one resurrected, the experience would be like walking through a doorway out of the present wicked system of things into the righteous, orderly new system of things.

¹⁸ Of course, the person who died many years ago will be surprised to find circumstances on earth so different. He will have to be informed by the members of the "great crowd" of the works that God has performed in the meantime, particularly in giving His Son as the atonement sacrifice. He will also learn how the good conditions are a result of Christ's Kingdom rule. It would be in harmony with God's loving-kindness to assume that family members and friends will be able to receive back their dead loved ones, just as was the case with resurrections reported in the Bible. (Luke 7:12-15; 8:49-56; Hebrews 11:35) Then, after a period of training, the resurrected ones will, in turn, be able to receive and help their yet dead loved ones who are subsequently brought back. Thus no one will be resurrected to a totally unfamiliar world, but, rather, to warm companionship, with no 'communication

17. If a person died centuries ago, will it seem to him that a long time has passed between his death and his resurrection? 18. (a) What will the resurrected ones have to learn? (b) Logically, how will those who are resurrected not be brought back to a totally unfamiliar world, with a 'communication gap'?

gap.' This process will continue until all the ransomed dead are finally resurrected. What a joyous time that will be!

GOD BECOMES "ALL THINGS TO EVERYONE"

[19] At the end of the thousand years, the last trace of sin and its consequence, death, will have been destroyed. (1 Corinthians 15:26) But does this reaching of perfection by all then on earth mean that such persons cannot sin? No, for the Bible reveals that persons reaching that state will not be assured of *everlasting* life until they prove faithful against a final attack by Satan the Devil. When Christ's kingdom and priesthood accomplish the restoration to perfection, Christ turns the Kingdom back to God, and man again stands in relation to God as Adam did. The situation is restored as it was at the beginning and each man's final, everlasting destiny is for God alone to determine. God permits this attack by Satan and his demon hosts.

[20] Revelation 20:7-10 describes what occurs as a test on earth's inhabitants: "Now as soon as the thousand years have been ended, Satan will be let loose out of his prison [the abyss, where he had been placed just before the thousand years began], and he will go out to mislead those nations in the four corners of the earth, Gog and Magog, to gather them together for the war. The number of these is as the sand of the sea [an unstated, hence humanly undeterminable number]. And they advanced over the breadth of the earth and encircled the camp of the holy ones and the beloved

19. Though perfection comes by Christ's thousand-year rule, when will those on earth be granted everlasting life?
20. What test will come upon the perfect inhabitants of the earth at the end of the thousand years?

city. But fire came down out of heaven and devoured them. And the Devil who was misleading them was hurled into the lake of fire and sulphur, where both the wild beast and the false prophet already were; and they will be tormented day and night forever and ever."—Compare Revelation 20:1-3.

²¹ This prophecy shows that some of the people then on earth will group themselves to attack the faithful ones on earth. They will be induced to do so by Satan and his demons. Why would perfect persons do this? Just as Adam and Eve did, they step out for independence from God. They are convinced that here is the *opportunity* to do this. Satan thus makes a 'last stand' to win his fight over the great issue that he originally raised, namely, the issue of the rightness of God's rulership. He fails, for the faithful ones, who doubtless constitute the great majority of mankind, remain firm. Then Satan and those following him are hurled into the "lake of fire." This is the "second death," where, to all eternity, they are held in 'torment' (jailers were in olden times called "tormentors" [Matthew 18:34, *Authorized Version*]). They are 'locked up' in nonexistence forever.

²² Those who faithfully stood firm for God's rulership or sovereignty will then be granted *everlasting life.* They will "come to life," that is, *real* assured life. (Revelation 20:4-6) Thus God becomes "all things to everyone." (1 Corinthians 15:28) But how can God safely guarantee that

21. (a) What issue will again be raised? (b) What will be the outcome?
22. (a) How can God safely guarantee everlasting life on earth to those who remain faithful under the final test? (b) What example do we have that God can know a person so thoroughly that he can be sure the person will never sin?

these will live forever? Because he thoroughly knows who those are who love him and who would never turn away from him. We have an example of this ability of God in the case of Jesus Christ, whom God knew so thoroughly and completely that he could foretell that Christ would be faithful through every test. God even had his prophets write in advance many of the very details of things that Christ would do in obedience to God under severe hardships.—Isaiah 53:7, 11; Psalms 40:7-10; 45:7.

GOD'S PURPOSE TOWARD EARTH FULFILLED

23 So, although it has taken time, God's purpose toward the earth will be gloriously fulfilled. Earth will be a grand paradise, filled with humans praising God and showing love to one another. But will the earth then become too crowded? No. We can be sure that God knows the number of persons that can comfortably live on earth. So he can reserve plenty of space for mountains and seas as well as room for the habitation of wildlife, for beauty and recreation. He will adjust matters so that there will be no feeling of crowding as is the case in large cities today. Life will be enjoyable, with all persons in harmony. Yet, since they will vary in personality and in gifts or talents and skills, there will be endless vistas of interest and delight to be enjoyed in their company. The many fields of activity will provide absorbing study, research and enterprise, with a real, lasting purpose. Each individual will be able to contribute his talents and abilities for the common welfare,

---

23. How will there be enjoyment of life, with full opportunity for exercise of talents and abilities for the welfare of all on earth?

and will have the energy and time to do so.
—Compare Isaiah 40:29-31 and the principle expressed at Ecclesiastes 5:18-20.

²⁴ When God created man and woman, he told them to subdue the earth and to exercise dominion over the animal creation. (Genesis 1:28) The earth was made as a gift to man—his home. (Psalm 115:16) Man will therefore know how to take care of the earth, exercising proper, loving control over the animals. The animals will be man's friends and will instinctively respect his dominion. God demonstrated this when he restored ancient Israel from exile in Babylon. (Hosea 2:18) In full possession of his faculties, with alertness of all his senses, a man will have no serious accidents. Look at the animals in their natural habitat. The bat, with his "sonar" equipment, flies in the dark, unerringly avoiding objects even as fine as a piano wire. A bird comes in to a perfect landing on a limb or twig. They are equipped fully for the life they live, and they enjoy living. With stronger reasoning we can be assured that man, being superior to the animals, will be perfectly at home in his environment.

²⁵ Work will then be joyful. Man will not have to eat bread 'in the sweat of his face,' as Adam was told after he had sinned. (Genesis 3:19) Work and the exercise of all their faculties will keep humans occupied in worthwhile, purposeful pursuits. As foreshadowed in ancient Israel when they obeyed the Law, there will be ample allowance of time for association with one's nearest

24. (a) What will then be man's relationship to the animals?
(b) Will serious accidents occur?
25. Why will life then never become boring or monotonous?

and most intimate ones, as well as for becoming acquainted with new friends. So in all the earth, one will have friends who will always remain friends. All of this will come from making friends with those who love humankind most, Jehovah God and his Son Jesus Christ.—John 15:14.

Chapter 16

You Can Be Confident
of a Reward

LIFE is a gift from God. No one would have life at all had not God, because of his own generosity, created the first man and woman. (Revelation 4:11) Being sinful people, we would not be here if God had not patiently 'put up' with our ways. "If errors were what you watch, O Jah, O Jehovah, who could stand?" wrote the psalmist. —Psalm 130:3.

2 Life is indeed a *free gift*. And it is God's will that the human race keep on living. (1 Timothy 2:3, 4) He gave mankind, not mere life, but life with a *purpose*. God does not grant everlasting life to his enemies, because they would only cause disorder in the earth and harm to others. Therefore our obtaining everlasting life is dependent on our faith in God, which really means that we must be friends of God. "Without faith it is impossible to please him well, for he that approaches

---

1. Whom can we thank for our being here on earth?
2. Though life is a free gift, on what does continued life depend?

God must believe that he is and that he becomes the rewarder of those earnestly seeking him." —Hebrews 11:6.

³ Our faith, then, gains the friendship of God, and this friendship means a reward. In your study of the Bible, as you are doing, you are actually seeking him—that is, seeking to know him, to please him and become friends with him. And as you learn more about him your faith will become stronger, more solidly founded. —2 Peter 1:5-8.

⁴ You may wonder, 'Why have I been able to see these things about God's purposes when many of my friends and acquaintances do not see them?' You can indeed be happy that you do, because out of millions of persons, God has seen fit to let you know about his purpose. He draws to him whomever he wants to, but not arbitrarily or without good reason. We cannot see what God sees. God reveals his secrets to those who have a sincerely inquiring mind to know about him, as Jesus pointed out. (Matthew 13:10-15) And he knows just when circumstances are right for the individual to see and grasp the truth of the good news. (Acts 8:25-36) God's choice of friends is right. He does not make mistakes. Therefore you can be assured that an opportunity for everlasting life is opened to you.—Acts 13:48.

⁵ Jehovah God sees hearts. He blesses those who use their reasoning power and look sincerely into his Word. He appreciates and favors those who do even the slightest service toward him,

---

3. What is the main purpose in studying the Bible?
4. If you are sincerely seeking God by studying his Word, of what can you be assured?
5. What loving appreciation does God show toward those sincerely seeking him?

giving them further opportunities to know him.
—Matthew 10:40-42.

⁶ However, the apostle Paul warned: "Working
together with him, we also entreat you not to
accept the undeserved kindness of God and miss
its purpose." (2 Corinthians 6:1) It is up to the
one whom God has favored with his kindness to
appreciate it and to go ahead and come to establish
a real, lasting relationship with him. (2 Corinthians 6:2) What a pity for one who, receiving
God's favor, turns away and loses out on the
fine reward!—Proverbs 4:5-9.

PERSONAL PURPOSE IN LIFE NOW

⁷ As you have considered God's Word thus far
as to his purpose, the truth may be clear that your
own life also indeed DOES HAVE A PURPOSE.
The will of God is that we conform our life to
his purpose because only God's wisdom and guidance can bring us to a desirable, happy goal. A
man or woman may set out to accomplish a purpose with good intentions, and that purpose may
appear to succeed for a while. But if it has no
regard for God's direction it will end only in
frustration. Such a person will actually be out of
harmony with the rest of God's creation.

⁸ The apostle Paul wrote to the young man
Timothy, showing the reason for making the pur-
suit of God's ways our own purpose. He said:
"In a large house there are vessels [utensils] not
only of gold and silver but also of wood and
earthenware, and some for an honorable purpose

6. Why should we not undervalue or look down on the opportunities that God opens up for us to know him?
7. (a) From what we have studied, what may we conclude?
(b) What will happen if a person pursues a purpose in life
that disregards God's will?
8, 9. What will be the outcome for one who goes through life
without a purpose?

but others for a purpose lacking honor. If, therefore, anyone keeps clear of the latter ones, he will be a vessel for an honorable purpose, sanctified, useful to his owner [Jehovah God bought all humankind through the sacrifice of his Son], prepared for every good work."—2 Timothy 2:20, 21.

⁹ But without a purpose in life a person in this world will be easy prey to bad influences, "tossed about as by waves and carried hither and thither by every wind of teaching by means of the trickery of men, by means of cunning in contriving error." (Ephesians 4:14) He will become a vessel for a purpose lacking honor.

BAPTISM, A SERIOUS BUT ESSENTIAL STEP

¹⁰ After learning and determining what God's will is, and after making a dedication of yourself through Christ to do God's will forever, you may be baptized in water. This step is very serious. You must be *sure* that this is the course you want to take. You are thereby imitating Jesus' example and obeying his command. Baptism is essential for one to become a follower of Jesus Christ. (Hebrews 10:7; Matthew 3:13-15; 28:19, 20) In being baptized, you are publicly declaring that your purpose in life is to serve God fully as his will and purpose are made known to you. *Make your own decision.* You should not be baptized because you let someone "push" you, or just because someone else gets baptized.

¹¹ Now, baptism in symbol of your dedication is but a beginning of your Christian course. Regardless of what education or position you have

---

10. When should a person be baptized?
11. Should a newly baptized person feel that now he (or she) is in no need of further counsel or help? Why?

had in the world, you are, Scripturally, a spiritual "babe." It is absolutely essential that you keep on studying, continuing to get help from those who are serving God. (1 Corinthians 14:20) You need regular association with the Christian congregation. Do not try to 'go it' on your own. —Hebrews 10:24, 25.

¹² Time 'in the truth' is not the sole barometer of your spirituality. Continued study and application of the Bible's principles are also necessary to produce the fruits that indicate maturity. (Hebrews 5:14; Romans 12:1, 2) The apostle Paul made these points clear to the early Hebrew Christians. He told them: "Indeed, although you ought to be teachers in view of the time, you again need someone to teach you from the beginning the elementary things of the sacred pronouncements of God; and you have become such as need milk, not solid food." He counseled them: "Let us press on to maturity."—Hebrews 5:12; 6:1.

LOOKING FOR REWARD NOT SELFISH

¹³ In pursuing a purpose in life as a follower of Jesus Christ it is entirely proper, and not selfish, to look for God to reward you for faithfulness to him. (Colossians 3:24) Jehovah wants us to know that he is the kind of God that rewards those who love him. He is not like many worldly persons who have no appreciation or consideration for those who do things in love or loyalty. And a god without appreciation and loyalty, who never rewarded his servants, would be unworthy of worship. But Jehovah God is loyal;

12. Does being a long time 'in the truth' in itself mean that one is a mature Christian? Why?
13. Is it selfish to serve God with a reward in view? Explain.

he is warmhearted and draws close to his friends. (Jeremiah 3:12) Even if you should make a bad mistake, entreat his forgiveness in prayer. (1 John 1:9; 2:1, 2; Luke 18:1-8) Seek help from fellow Christians. (James 5:16-18) If you hold fast to faith in him, he "will by no means leave you nor by any means forsake you."—Hebrews 13:5, 6.

¹⁴ However, Jesus said that, on our part, we should not feel that we are doing God a "favor," or *earning* life as wages by serving him. He told his disciples: "When you have done all the things assigned to you, say, 'We are good-for-nothing slaves. What we have done is what we ought to have done.'" (Luke 17:10) Nonetheless, we know that God loves us and does not feel that our efforts are of no value to him.

¹⁵ So there are great rewards to look forward to, of things far beyond what we are able to conceive. Our keeping of faithfulness to God gives, first of all, a better life *now,* with a purpose. (1 Timothy 4:8) Then, there is the prospect of being a part of the "foundation" of the "new earth." What a joy to be in on the "groundwork" of making the earth a paradise! More than that, how fine to be on hand to receive people back in the resurrection and to teach, help and train them! There is a fine purpose in the *life ahead!*

¹⁶ But do not belittle the marvelous opportunity you have to serve God *now.* For this is the last time that people will have an opportunity to stand for God's side of the issue of universal rulership *amid a whole world of people who do not know God's provisions.* Furthermore, it is the last op-

14. Even if we come to serve God with all our might, what should be our attitude?
15. What rewards does faithfulness bring now and in the future?
16. Why is it such a great privilege to serve God now?

portunity to proclaim the good news to such people under conditions of opposition. What a fine way to *prove* your loyalty to God! (Matthew 24:14) Doing this brings the greatest reward. Now is the opportunity to work together with "God's household, which is the congregation of the living God, a pillar and support of the truth," in sharing and proclaiming the good news of the Kingdom to others.—1 Timothy 3:15.

DO NOT BE DISMAYED BY OPPOSITION

[17] You can associate with this congregation where God has "deposited" the truth about himself and his purposes. But when you try to put the truth of God's Word into effect in your life and to speak the truth, do not be surprised or dismayed when opposition faces you. The apostle Peter gave these comforting words: "Beloved ones, do not be puzzled at the burning among you, which is happening to you for a trial, as though a strange thing were befalling you. On the contrary, go on rejoicing forasmuch as you are sharers in the sufferings of the Christ, that you may rejoice and be overjoyed also during the revelation of his glory. If you are being reproached for the name of Christ, you are happy, because the spirit of glory, even the spirit of God, is resting upon you."—1 Peter 4:12-14.

[18] A good thing to do when faced with opposition is to look back at your former state—your life and attitude before coming to a knowledge of God's purposes. This will help you to be sympa-

---

17. Why may opposition be expected, and how should you view it?
18. (a) How can you develop more sympathy for those who oppose you? (b) Should you feel that those who oppose you are absolutely "wicked"? (c) Even if treated harshly, what should your response be?

thetic with the situation of those who oppose you and to have compassion for them. You may see that formerly, in your ignorance of God's ways, you also did many of the wrong things that they are doing now. You may even have had a bad attitude toward God, toward the Bible and toward those who are witnesses for Jehovah God. (Compare Colossians 3:5-7.) By looking at the way you felt then, you can avoid the feeling that these people are absolutely "wicked" because they do not listen. You will not be condemning them or giving them up as hopeless. When someone, even in a harsh manner, challenges your faith, you will be "always ready to make a defense before everyone that demands of you a reason for the hope in you, but doing so together *with a mild temper and deep respect.*"—1 Peter 3:15.

AVOID BEING 'OVER-RIGHTEOUS'

[19] There is a certain temptation for one who sees the right way of life to become "righteous overmuch." He may tend toward his being a "perfectionist." This may lead him to begin to be critical of others, to look down on them, and to become a judge of his fellowman. (Ecclesiastes 7:16; Matthew 7:1, 2) He may grow to have the feeling that he is *just a little better* than those who do not yet know the truth. But it must be kept in mind that Christ died for *all mankind. You* are one of them and, without his help, you would be like the rest. Jesus Christ has compassion for all. He knows that circumstances, and the spirit of this world under its god Satan, have forced many people into a bad way of life. It was

---

19. (a) How might a person fall into the snare of being 'over-righteous'? (b) Rather than feeling that you are better than those not serving God, what should you realize and do?

prophetically said: "Darkness itself will cover the earth, and thick gloom the national groups." This is true today. (Isaiah 60:2) Therefore it is necessary to have understanding and sympathy and have as our aim to *help* rather than accuse or condemn.—1 Thessalonians 2:7, 8.

²⁰ Accordingly, a husband or wife coming to a knowledge of the truth should put stress on making himself or herself a *better* husband or wife. A child should become a better, more obedient child. This may have much more influence on others than words do. While all persons receiving the truth should be enthusiastic and zealous, it must be recognized that any attempt to "push" the unbelieving mate, the relative or friend may actually push him or her away from listening. Do not "nag" a person because he has a habit or belief of which you do not approve. Rather, use patience and more than the usual kindness. Even toward those showing enmity, be "cautious as serpents and yet innocent as doves," using every possible means, in love, to help others to see the truth. (Matthew 10:16; 1 Corinthians 9:20, 23) Whether you are a wife, a husband or a child, follow the principle expressed by the apostle Peter at 1 Peter 3:1, 2:

²¹ "In like manner, you wives, be in subjection to your own husbands, in order that, if any are not obedient to the word, they may be won *without a word through the conduct* of their wives, because of having been eyewitnesses of your chaste conduct together with deep respect."

20, 21. What principle and course of action should a person employ toward those closely associated with him (or her)?

BE A HAPPY INTEGRITY KEEPER

[22] During your life course as a Christian, things will not always go just right for you, because we are not yet in God's new system of things. Your efforts to apply Bible principles will not always completely solve or remove your problems. But they will help you greatly to cope with these problems. They will enable you to do all that can be done to make such less troublesome. So, if things occur that trouble you, do not become a complainer. Rather, be happy. Rejoice in the truth. Realize that Adam's sin and Satan's influence as the "god of this system of things" are the cause; God is not.—2 Corinthians 4:4.

[23] So, instead of complaining at hardships or undesirable occurrences that you presumed would not happen among God's people, take advantage of the opportunity to show that you are like Christ, an integrity keeper. Vindicate Jehovah's name by demonstrating that not all men will let difficulties turn them away from God, as the Devil charged, but that they can be integrity keepers.

[24] What a rewarding purpose life has indeed! With all the worthwhile things that we can do now, using what "gifts" or abilities we have to honor God and to help our fellowman, there is a real satisfaction in living—we find *our place* in life. And God, in using us, does not ask us to

22. (a) Will your efforts to apply Bible principles always remove problems? (b) If things do not go just right for you, what attitude should you avoid?
23. If something bad should occur in the congregation of God's people, is this a reason to become discouraged, offended or disgruntled?
24. (a) How does our serving God give us a satisfactory purpose in living? (b) Can we count on continued purpose in life forever, with no dullness or monotony?

give up living a normal, productive life and become ascetics or in any way fanatical. Rather, he makes life better and more productive of things having lasting value. Furthermore, we will forever receive at God's hand new and exciting projects for accomplishment, so that life will become ever more purposeful, never monotonous. As the apostle Paul wrote to his Christian associates: "My God will fully supply all your need to the extent of his riches in glory by means of Christ Jesus." —Philippians 4:19; Psalm 145:16; Romans 8:38, 39.

DOES MAN'S SHORT LIFE-SPAN MAKE SENSE?

The 192-page book **Is This Life All There Is?** answers this and related questions, such as:

- ◆ **What about those who have already died?**
- ◆ **Where are the dead?**
- ◆ **Do the dead need your help?**
- ◆ **Can you talk with the dead?**
- ◆ **Can spiritism bring you comfort?**

This book **Is This Life All There Is?** may be obtained by sending 25c (U.S.) to **Watchtower**, using one of the addresses below.

ALASKA 99507: 2552 East 48th Ave., Anchorage. **AUSTRALIA:** 11 Beresford Road, Strathfield, N.S.W. 2135. **BAHAMAS:** Box N-1247, Nassau, N.P. **BARBADOS:** Fontabelle Rd., Bridgetown. **BELIZE:** Box 257, Belize City. **BRAZIL:** Rua Guaíra, 216, Bosque da Saúde, 04142 São Paulo, SP; Caixa Postal 12.896, 01000 São Paulo, SP. **CANADA M6A 1Z5:** 150 Bridgeland Ave., Toronto, Ont. **ENGLAND:** Watch Tower House, The Ridgeway, London NW7 1RN. **FIJI:** Box 23, Suva. **FRANCE:** 81 rue du Point-du-Jour, 92100 Boulogne-Billancourt. **GERMANY, FEDERAL REPUBLIC OF:** Postfach 5920, D-6200 Wiesbaden 1. **GHANA:** Box 760, Accra. **GUYANA:** 50 Brickdam, Georgetown 16. **HAWAII 96814:** 1228 Pensacola St., Honolulu. **HONG KONG:** 312 Prince Edward Rd., Second Floor, Kowloon. **INDIA:** South Avenue, Santa Cruz, Bombay 400054. **IRELAND:** 86 Lindsay Rd., Glasnevin, Dublin 9. **JAMAICA:** 41 Trafalgar Rd., Kingston 10. **KENYA:** Box 47788, Nairobi. **LEEWARD ISLANDS:** Box 119, St. Johns, Antigua. **LIBERIA:** P.O. Box 171, Monrovia. **MALAYSIA:** 20 Scotland Close, Penang. **NEWFOUNDLAND, CANADA A1C 2M1:** 239 Pennywell Rd., St. John's. **NEW ZEALAND:** 6-A Western Springs Rd., Auckland 3. **NIGERIA:** P.O. Box 194, Yaba, Lagos State. **PAKISTAN:** 8-E Habibullah Rd., Lahore 3. **PANAMA:** Apartado 1386, Panama 1. **PAPUA NEW GUINEA:** Box 113, Port Moresby. **PHILIPPINES, REPUBLIC OF:** P.O. Box 2044, Manila 2800; 186 Roosevelt Ave., San Francisco del Monte, Quezon City 3010. **PORTUGAL:** Apartado 21.022, Lisbon 2. **RHODESIA:** 35 Fife Avenue, Salisbury. **SIERRA LEONE:** Box 136, Freetown. **SOUTH AFRICA:** Private Bag 2, P.O. Elandsfontein, 1406. **SRI LANKA, REP. OF:** 62 Layard's Road, Colombo 5. **SWITZERLAND:** Ulmenweg 45; P.O. Box 477, CH-3601 Thun. **TRINIDAD:** 2 La Seiva Road, Maraval, Port of Spain. **UNITED STATES OF AMERICA:** 117 Adams St., Brooklyn, N.Y. 11201.